VOODOO OS/2

TIPS & TRICKS WITH AN ATTITUDE

For Versions 2.0 & 2.1

VOODOO OS/2

TIPS & TRICKS WITH AN ATTITUDE

For Versions 2.0 & 2.1

Allen G. Taylor

Ventana Press Voodoo™ Series

Voodoo OS/2: Tips & Tricks With An Attitude
For Versions 2.0 and 2.1
Copyright © 1993 by Allen G. Taylor
Ventana Press Voodoo™ Series

Library of Congress Cataloging-in-Publication Data
Taylor, Allen G.
    Voodoo OS/2 : tips & tricks with an attitude for versions 2.0 & 2.1 / Allen G. Taylor. -- 1st ed.
       p. cm. -- (Ventana voodoo series)
    Includes index.
    ISBN 1-56604-066-3
    1. Operating systems (Computers) 2. OS/2 (Computer file) I. Title. II. Series.
QA76.76.O63T388 1993
005.4'469--dc20
                                  93-29672
                                      CIP

Book design: Karen Wysocki
Cover design: Thea Tulloss, Tulloss Design
Index service: Dianne Bertsch, Answers Plus
Technical review: Bret Curran, Brian Curran
Editorial staff: John Cotterman, Jean Kaplan, Pam Richardson, Jessica Ryan
Production staff: John Cotterman, Marcia Webb

First Edition 9 8 7 6 5 4 3 2 1
Printed in the United States of America

Ventana Press, Inc.
P.O. Box 2468
Chapel Hill, NC 27515
919/942-0220
FAX 919/942-1140

Trademarks

Trademarked names appear throughout this book. Rather than list the names and entities that own the trademarks or insert a trademark symbol with each mention of the trademarked name, the publisher states that it is using the names only for editorial purposes and to the benefit of the trademark owner with no intention of infringing upon that trademark.

About the Author

Allen G. Taylor is president of Computer Power, a computing consulting firm in Portland, Oregon, specializing in system development, software design, database design and technology marketing. He is a bestselling author of over a dozen computer books including *File Format Handbook* (Microtrend), *ObjectVision 2.0 Developer's Guide* (Bantam), *Teach Yourself Paradox* (Henry Holt/MIS), *Unix Guide for DOS Users* (MIS) and *Understanding OS/2* (Scott Foresman).

Allen Taylor is also a nationally recognized speaker and adjunct professor of computing science at Linfield College.

Acknowledgments

Many people helped and encouraged me during the writing of this book. Without their help, I could not have written it. I would like to specifically thank the following very helpful people:

Tom Gallaudet
Bill Hinkle
David Kaaret
Gary Spoon
Matt Wagner
Wes Walterman
Benson Wills
David Wofford

Dedication

This book is dedicated to Joyce Carolyn Taylor who has added an element of mystery and magic to my life for the past twenty-six years.

TABLE OF CONTENTS

INTRODUCTION

You've heard that OS/2 delivers a much higher level of performance than is possible with Windows running on top of DOS. You've probably also heard that OS/2 is a 32-bit, multitasking operating system, which certainly distinguishes it from the 16-bit, single-tasking DOS/Windows combination. Does this increase in power mean that it is harder to understand and use? What does a person need to know to tap the power of OS/2, without becoming a power user?

With OS/2, a little voodoo will go a long way. With the tips in this book you can avoid the traps that often snare the unwary. This book can help you take control of the most powerful and solidly reliable operating system available for personal computers. You can modify the user interface to reflect your own preferences. You will learn the best ways to run DOS, Windows and OS/2 programs and to navigate the highly intuitive Workplace Shell. You'll also learn to deal with files, printing, useful mini-applications and the exciting new field of affordable multimedia.

This and other books in the Ventana Voodoo™ Series give quick answers to frequent questions that are not well-documented elsewhere. With *Voodoo OS/2* you'll learn to use OS/2 to accomplish more in less time and with less hassle.

WHAT'S INSIDE

Chapter 1: Gaining Control

This chapter gives you all you need to know to start OS/2, manage it while it is operating and shut it down gracefully without losing data. You master the basics of operating with windows and other objects on the OS/2 desktop. Such objects include menus, dialog boxes and a strong set of controls, each optimized for a particular task.

OS/2 offers several kinds of on-line help, and they are all explained here. With help on the screen and your copy of *Voodoo OS/2* at your side, you will rarely need to look at IBM's printed documentation.

Chapter 2: Personalizing Your Desktop

The standard, default version of OS/2 that you see when you power it up for the first time is very pleasing to the eye and easy on the hand. You may decide to leave the user interface just the way you found it. You don't have to, though. OS/2's flexibility permits you to change the way it looks and feels to more closely match your own personal preferences. You can change the mouse from right-handed to left-handed, change the speed with which the pointer tracks your hand movements and change the double-click interval. You can modify the keyboard with custom key assignments and change its repeat rate. You can create your own window backgrounds and replace standard system icons with ones that you draw yourself or pick from an icon library. Many of the not-so-obvious as well as the highly visible aspects of the user interface are potentially under your control.

Chapter 3: Getting Programs to Run

Programs originally written for DOS and Microsoft Windows, as well as those written specifically for OS/2, will all run under OS/2. In fact, several instances of each can run simultaneously. Learn the intricacies of concurrent operation and how to avoid problems that might arise. Shut down renegade programs without crashing the entire system and learn how memory size and swapping affect the way your programs run.

Chapter 4: The Workplace Shell

The Workplace Shell is that part of OS/2 that communicates directly with you. This chapter gets into the nitty gritty of how it works, what doesn't work, how you can set it up to your best advantage and how you can protect yourself from your own mistakes. The tricks of populating your WPS desktop with your customized objects are revealed, as is communication with WIN-OS/2 Windows 3.1 emulation.

Chapter 5: File Magic

OS/2 can use files created by DOS programs but supports a richer file structure itself. Learn the nuances of extended file attributes and the differences between FAT files and HPFS files. Explore the powerful setup notebook paradigm, which allows you to change file attributes without being a master of file formats. Associate data files with applications so that calling one automatically invokes the other. Discover the power and the convenience of accessing files through their shadows.

Chapter 6: Curse-Free Printing

Printing is one of those areas that can be simple or very complex. OS/2's multitasking capability gives you the flexibility to print multiple documents and perform other processing simultaneously. Understandably, this makes control a crucial issue. Tips in this chapter may reveal printing secrets you weren't aware of. The differences between screen fonts, printer fonts, bitmap fonts, outline fonts, TrueType fonts and ATM fonts are explained, giving the advantages and disadvantages of each.

Chapter 7: Productivity Programs

OS/2 2.1 includes 23 small programs (applets) designed to enhance your personal productivity. Some of them can be very handy indeed, and it pays to know what they can do for you. Included are a group of applications that, taken together, constitute a personal information manager. You can increase your personal efficiency greatly by applying these integrated applets in the proper way. This chapter tells how.

Chapter 8: Installation Magic

OS/2 is a resource-hungry operating system. In fact, it may require more resources than you have. Tips in this chapter tell you how to configure OS/2 so the capabilities you want are present, while un-needed features are not consuming resources. You can save time and money by making the right choices on hardware configuration and file system setup. Making OS/2 2.1 co-resident with Microsoft Windows NT is explained, allowing a head-to-head comparison.

Chapter 9: Multimedia Magic

Multimedia is an application area still in its infancy, but it will surely become standard on most personal computers within a few years. OS/2 2.1 provides applications in all the major facets of multimedia; this chapter tells you how to exploit them. Full motion video, combined with high fidelity music, speech and realistic sound effects are now available to anyone with a PC equipped with a sound card and a CD-ROM drive. Get the scoop here on how to effectively use OS/2's multimedia capabilities.

HOW TO USE THIS BOOK

If you don't have OS/2 yet, read through this book to get an idea of the kinds of things you can do with the operating system. You may decide that OS/2 is the way to go. If you are an OS/2 novice, this book can help you get the system up and running the way you want it. If you already have OS/2, you will find numerous hints in these pages that will help you conserve your most valuable resource: time.

Keep *Voodoo OS/2* around and browse through it again from time to time. Perhaps on your first reading an idea that is not of immediate relevance will be valuable to you later.

Conventions Used

To make it easy to correlate screen events with the book text, we use the same capitalization standards that IBM uses. Initial capital letters are used for all words in names of folders, menus, notebooks, tabs and buttons ("Startup folder," "Delete button"). Many menu, dialog box and notebook choices appear on your OS/2 desktop with a capital letter only on the first word ("Search all subfolders," "New name:"). We followed this convention and did not delineate the choices with quotation marks. As you follow the text with the screen shots this will become clear.

USE THE INDEX!

When you have a specific problem that needs an immediate answer, thumb through the index looking for references to keywords that are related to your topic of interest. Although a single chapter may be devoted to the general area of your question, OS/2 is so tightly integrated that relevant information may be found scattered throughout the book.

SOFTWARE VERSION

This book is written to address the features and capabilities of OS/2 version 2.1. Much of the material here also applies to version 2.0.

By the way, we mean no disrespect to anyone's religion or politics. "Voodoo" books are meant to be fun. They get your attention and are full of magic tricks. In the words of Arthur C. Clarke, "Any sufficiently advanced technology will appear to be magic to those at a lower technological level." For most people, computers are sufficiently advanced to qualify. This book will hopefully blow away some of the smoke and show some of the mirrors for what they are.

YOUR FAVORITE TRICK

If you have a tip or favorite trick that is not covered here, send it to Ventana Press or to me for inclusion in the next edition. If we include your trick, the next edition is yours free. Be sure to include your name and address.

If you like this book, stay on the lookout for other Ventana Press Voodoo™ books. They are designed to help you make magic with the most popular software on the market today.

You can write to Ventana Press, P.O. Box 2468, Chapel Hill, NC 27515, (919) 942-0220 or fax (919) 942-1140, or reach me on CompuServe (72607,507).

> —*Allen G. Taylor*
> P.O. Box 230097
> Portland, OR 97281-0097
> Compuserve: 72607,507
> Internet: allent@linfield.edu

Chapter 1
GAINING CONTROL

Voodoo is secret knowledge that only initiates possess, giving them control over powerful forces that are mysterious and incomprehensible to the rest of humanity. This book is your admission ticket into that exclusive fraternity of people who not only understand OS/2, but can use it effectively to achieve their objectives faster and easier than with other operating environments.

OS/2 is the first 32-bit multithreaded, multitasking operating system available on IBM-compatible personal computers. This sounds like voodoo already, but is really quite simple. *Multitasking* means that a system can work on several different functions at the same time. This capability improves performance because more parts of the system hardware are in use more of the time. A single-tasking operating system (such as DOS) uses only one part of the system at a time, leaving the rest idle. *Multithreaded* means that the division of labor is taking place at a very low level. Multiple "threads" of execution are flowing simultaneously. Multithreaded multitasking operating systems can deliver significantly better performance than can single-threaded multitasking operating systems, which in turn outperform single tasking operating systems. The fact that OS/2 is a 32-bit operating system means that it takes full advantage of the hardware built into the Intel 80386, 80486, Pentium and compatible processors.

The current release of OS/2, version 2.1, is often compared to Microsoft Windows 3.1, but is different in several important ways.

- **OS/2 is a true operating system.** It was designed, from top to bottom, as an efficient yet feature-rich means of putting the capabilities of the hardware at the service of application programs and users. Windows 3.1 (and its successor Windows 4.0) is not an operating system but rather a layer of software that rides on top of the DOS operating system. It is not an integral part of DOS but was added to give DOS a graphical look and feel. The DOS/Windows combination must cope with the intrinsic deficiencies of an operating system that has its roots at the dawn of the personal computer era, when machines were much less powerful than they are today. Programmers appreciate the difference. They can build more powerful applications with OS/2.

- **OS/2 is a more reliable environment.** It allows you to logically isolate each application from all others running at the same time, as well as from the operating system. If one of those applications starts producing errors, it will not adversely affect OS/2 or the other active applications. In the worst case, it will gracefully die, allowing you to continue running the rest of your applications. Since Windows lacks that kind of protection, it can "freeze up" if a similar error occurs with one of its applications. Sometimes hitting the Reset button and starting from scratch is the only way to recover from such a problem in Windows.

- **OS/2, a 32-bit operating system, has an intrinsic performance advantage over DOS/Windows, a 16-bit environment.** Since OS/2 can handle data in 32-bit chunks rather than the 16-bit chunks that DOS can handle, compute-intensive tasks that can take advantage of 32-bit arithmetic run much more quickly under OS/2 than they do on the same hardware running DOS/Windows. This advantage is even more pronounced when running on systems with a 32-bit bus, such as computers with a MicroChannel or EISA bus.

Most programs that were designed to run under either DOS or Windows 3.1 will run under OS/2. OS/2 includes a DOS emulator and a Windows 3.1 emulator named WIN-OS/2. Well-behaved DOS and Windows programs (those that follow the rules promulgated by Microsoft) will run under OS/2.

Some DOS programs, particularly those that bypass DOS and control the hardware directly, will not run properly under OS/2. Disk management utilities, virus detection programs and games often bypass the operating system to control the hardware.

OS/2 can run multiple DOS sessions and multiple Windows sessions at the same time. Real DOS and Windows are single-tasking and cannot.

LAUNCHING OS/2

The OS/2 user is much like the captain of a seagoing vessel. There are three primary things to be concerned about: launching, navigating and docking. The sea captain who wishes to reach the destination port must first move away from the dock, negotiate the harbor and reach the sea without mishap. From there navigation becomes the key activity, since of all the places where the ship might end up (reefs, beaches, rocky coastlines, other ports), only one is the correct one. Finally, after visiting all the planned ports of call, the captain must successfully ease the ship into its berth back at the home port.

OS/2 must also be "launched," and there are several ways of doing it. Only one of them will be appropriate for the computer you are using. Once OS/2 is running, you must know how to "navigate" among the many "ports of call" (applications) that are available. Finally, since OS/2 is a multitasking operating system, with several things going on all the time, it is not enough to finish work on the last application and then turn off the computer. You must allow OS/2 to perform its shutdown procedure to make sure that no important data is lost or corrupted.

There are three different ways that OS/2 may be installed on a computer. Each one of these has its own way of launching the system. The method of launch depends on how many different operating systems you want to be able to use.

Launch Method #1: OS/2 is the Only Operating System Present

This is the easiest case. If OS/2 is the only operating system on the hard disk from which your system boots, it will automatically come up when your computer is turned on or rebooted. The appearance OS/2 will exhibit when it comes up depends on its state the last time it was shut down. If none of the DOS, Windows or OS/2 command prompt interfaces were active, the Workplace Shell (WPS) will fill the screen. If any of the DOS or OS/2 command prompt interfaces or the Windows desktop were active, they will be displayed.

Launching OS/2 on a single operating system (OS) computer is easy. If OS/2 has been installed on a computer and has previously been used by other people, all you have to do to launch it is to turn the computer on. The Workplace Shell will appear on the screen, looking something like Figure 1-1.

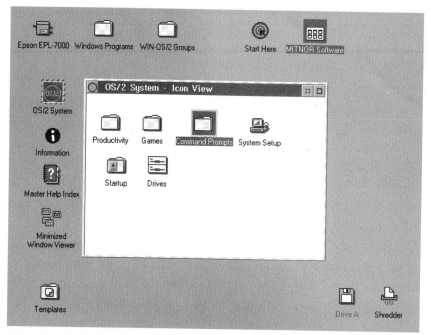

Figure 1-1: The Workplace Shell.

OS/2 remembers which windows were open and which applications were active the last time it was shut down.
If one or more of the command prompt interfaces or WIN-OS/2 was active but minimized the last time the system was used, you may not have realized it was operating. The next time OS/2 is booted, these interfaces will be fully displayed on screen rather than being minimized. You will have to minimize them again or, better yet, close them to remove the clutter from the desktop.

Keep several user interfaces active. If you are going to be switching between the OS/2 desktop, WIN-OS/2, and one of the command prompt interfaces frequently, it makes sense to invest some system resources to keep these interfaces active. Instead of closing WIN-OS/2, just minimize it and select the next object to work with from the OS/2 desktop. You can switch back to WIN-OS/2 instantaneously rather than having to wait for it to load from disk every time.

Launch Method #2: DOS is Present as Well as OS/2

If a DOS system is already present on the boot hard disk when OS/2 is installed, the OS/2 setup program will ask if you want to automatically create a Dual-Boot configuration. If you do, OS/2 will be placed into the same disk partition as DOS. Thereafter the system will boot up under OS/2. If you want to run native DOS (rather than OS/2's DOS emulation) use the BOOT command from the OS/2 command prompt to shut down OS/2 and boot DOS. When running under DOS you can use the BOOT command to shut down DOS and boot OS/2.

If your system is configured for Dual-Boot, the OS/2 boot drive must be configured according to the FAT (File Allocation Table) file management system rather than the HPFS (High Performance File System), since DOS is capable of using only the FAT system.

A characteristic of Dual-Boot is that all your files are available to both operating systems. DOS compatible programs and data may be used by either DOS or OS/2 as you choose.

To give you the Dual-Boot capability, OS/2 modifies the boot sector of your hard disk every time you switch operating systems. If you have switched operating systems even once, some virus detection systems will erroneously interpret this as an invasion by a hostile virus and issue a warning.

Launch Method #3: OS/2 is One of as Many as Three Operating Systems

When using the Boot Manager at installation, the boot hard disk is divided into as many as four partitions. One contains Boot Manager itself (1 MB), while the other three may each contain a different operating system. In this configuration, since one bootable partition cannot share files with another, files on the DOS logical boot drive are not accessible from OS/2. Conversely, files on the OS/2 logical boot drive are not accessible to DOS. However, if you have made one of your four partitions a non-bootable FAT volume (an extended partition), it will be accessible to both DOS and OS/2.

 Put any files you want to access from both DOS and OS/2 on a non-bootable FAT configured logical drive.

If you actually want to have three different operating systems—such as DOS 6.0, OS/2 2.1 and SCO UNIX or DOS 6.0, OS/2 1.3 and OS/2 2.1—none of them may share files with any of the others. Since all four partitions are bootable primary partitions, there is no place for a non-bootable FAT volume that would be accessible from the other partitions.

NAVIGATING AROUND OS/2

OS/2 has an object-oriented graphical user interface that makes extensive use of icons in the performance of operations. There is a reduced reliance on making menu selections and increased use of visual metaphors. For example, the Master Help Index is in the form of a notebook, with tabs that help you quickly flip to the "page" you want. You can create your own objects of various types using the templates provided, customizing them once they have been created.

A folder is an object that can contain other objects, such as applications. When you create a new object, you can place it into a folder or directly on the desktop, which is itself a folder although a special one. Folders can be placed within folders to any level of nesting.

The OS/2 System Window

Each icon displayed on the desktop represents an object, which can be a hardware device (such as a printer or disk drive), an OS/2 system object or an application object. The OS/2 System window is also displayed. Because objects can contain other objects it is possible to organize things in a convenient, easy-to-understand, hierarchical fashion. If you double-click mouse button 1 on an icon, its corresponding window is displayed. The OS/2 System window shown in Figure 1-1 contains folders and icons. Each folder contains a group of related objects. Some of these objects are useful features and applications that come with OS/2. Others could be applications that were installed later. We will be looking at the OS/2 objects that help us to work faster and with less effort.

Mice compatible with OS/2 may have either two or three buttons, which, when pressed, may cause actions. In this book we will refer to the button on the left as button 1. It is the one that is used most often, so it would be under the index finger of right-handed people. We will call the button on the right button 2.

The OS/2 System window contains folders named Productivity, Games, Command Prompts and Startup. It also holds the System Setup and Drives icons. You use System Setup to change aspects of the OS/2 environment. The Drives icon gives you a structured view of the contents of all the disk drives (floppy, hard and optical) on the system.

Select the application you want to work with by double-clicking on its icon on the desktop. If it is inside a folder instead of directly on the desktop, double-click on the folder icon to open the folder window, then double-click on the application icon inside it. If you use an application frequently you may want to copy it to the desktop. You can do so by following the procedure given in Chapter 4, "The Workplace Shell."

DOCKING OS/2

Just as a ship must be brought safely beside the dock and the engines shut down before a sea voyage is truly over, OS/2 must be properly shut down. In a single-user system such as DOS, as soon as you have completed the task at hand, you can push your computer's OFF button and walk away. Not so with a multitasking OS such as OS/2. There are other processes (the Workplace Shell for instance) that should be gracefully brought to a halt rather than being deprived of electricity while they are still active.

To shut down OS/2 properly, click your mouse button 2 anywhere on the desktop where there is *not* an icon. This displays the Desktop's System Menu (more about menus later in this chapter) as shown in Figure 1-2.

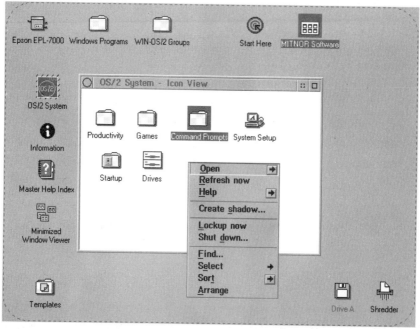

Figure 1-2: The Desktop System Menu, showing the Shut down... option.

Forgetting shutdown can cost you plenty. What if you don't shut down properly? Any files that are open when power is removed may be corrupted or may not retain the last changes that were made to them. This may result in unpredictable behavior the next time you use the system. Even worse, it may *not* manifest itself immediately. You might continue to rely on a corrupted system that could eventually die on you, taking with it the work you have done since the improper shut down.

OS/2 WINDOW BASICS

Let's use the OS/2 System window to help explain the components of OS/2 windows and how to operate on them. Other windows, which can be created by OS/2, applications or the user, will have the same general characteristics.

OS/2's Workplace Shell, which creates and displays the OS/2 graphical user interface, adheres to the Common User Access (CUA) standard. This standard is rather broad, so two products with quite different appearances (such as OS/2 2.1 and Windows 3.1) can both be fully compliant with it. One thing it specifies is that anything that can be done with a mouse or similar pointing device can also be done from the keyboard. If for any reason a mouse is not available, users can still operate the system.

You can swap the functions of the left and right mouse buttons. Some left-handed people may wish to manipulate the mouse with their left hand. In that case, the functions of button 1 and button 2 can be switched, so the button used most often is under the index finger of the left hand. Whether you use the right-handed or left-handed convention, the button 1/button 2 nomenclature will apply equally well. The middle button of three-button mice is not used by OS/2 but is used by some OS/2-compatible applications.

Use the mouse whenever possible. Although OS/2's CUA compliance tells us that you can do from the keyboard anything that you can do with a mouse, for most people the mouse is much easier to use. You can generally accomplish an operation several times faster with a mouse than you can from the keyboard, and mouse use is more intuitive. You do not have to memorize sequences of keystrokes.

Back up your mouse. Most of the mice available today have moving parts and thus are susceptible to failure. To assure that your work will not be interrupted by a mouse failure, buy a backup mouse (they are quite inexpensive). Test it to make sure it works, then put it on the shelf until you need it.

OS/2 can run several tasks at once, the maximum number depending on how much memory your machine has. To keep track of them, you can display on the screen a window for each one. Each window provides a view of an application that is currently running. Collections of applications (folders) or other objects can also be displayed in windows. Although several windows may be displayed on the screen at a time, only one has the *focus*. The application running in the window with the focus may accept input from the user. Other applications running at the same time may not. To interact with one of these other applications, the user must switch the focus to its window, making it the new active window.

There are several ways to shift the focus to a window that is already open, but the simplest is to put the mouse pointer somewhere within the window, then click mouse button 1. The active window has a title bar and a border that are different colors than the title bar and border of the inactive windows. Thus you can tell at a glance which window currently has the focus.

Bring hidden windows to the top of the desk. Sometimes the window to which you want to switch the focus may be completely obscured by one or more other windows that lie on top of it. In that case you can bring it to the top by clicking on its icon again.

Figure 1-3 shows the OS/2 desktop with a second window (the
Windows Programs window) covering the OS/2 System window.

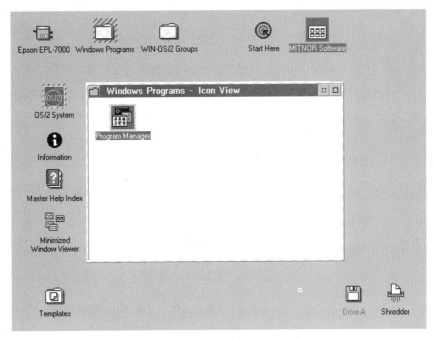

Figure 1-3: The OS/2 System window is hidden from view.

Notice that the OS/2 System icon, on the left edge of the desktop, has been "grayed out" with diagonal lines, indicating that it is
running. Double-clicking on the OS/2 System icon brings the OS/2
System window back to the foreground (Figure 1-4).

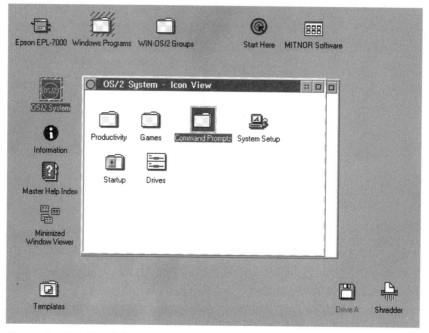

Figure 1-4: Double-clicking on the OS/2 System icon brings its window to the top.

Since it has just been activated with a double-click, the OS/2 System window is now the active window. Its title bar is darker than the title bar of the other visible window, its border is a different color and the other window is now partially obscured by the OS/2 System window.

Another way of switching the focus is by repeatedly pressing Alt-Tab. This cycles the focus through all open windows. Just keep pressing Alt-Tab until the window you want is on top.

Since it is not only possible but normal for several applications to be operating simultaneously, the user needs some way of monitoring the status of each one. OS/2 provides this ability by starting a *process* for each application and assigning each process a window. The windows for all currently active processes may or may not be visible on the screen at any given time. The user may select which windows are displayed and their size and location on the desktop.

A window is made up of a *client area* and a collection of *widgets*. The client area, taking up the bulk of the window, is where the actual contents of the window are displayed. Widgets are simple tools, located at or near the window border, that perform a function or allow you to change the appearance of the window.

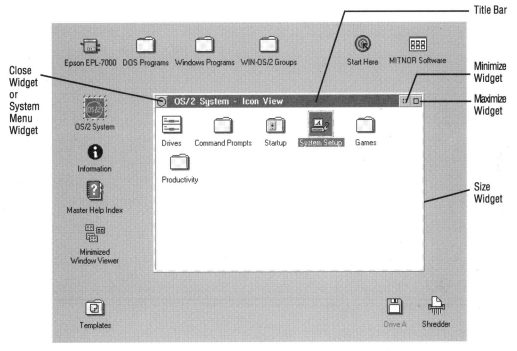

Figure 1-5: The desktop, pointing out the widgets located near the border of a typical window.

Moving & Sizing Windows

Any object on the OS/2 desktop that has a *title bar* (such as a window) can be moved. The title bar spans the top of the window as shown in Figure 1-5. To move a window, place the mouse pointer anywhere within the title bar, then press button 1. With button 1 still pressed, move the mouse pointer to the new location for the window. This has the effect of "dragging" the window to the new location. When you release button 1, the move is complete. Figure 1-6 shows the same desktop illustrated in Figure 1-5 after the displayed window has been dragged to a new location.

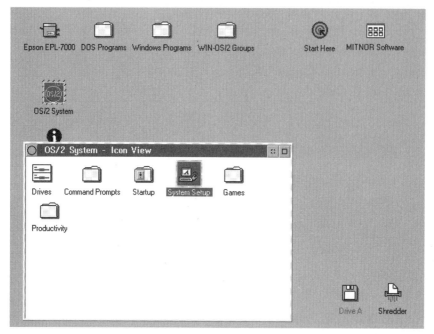

Figure 1-6: Desktop, after the OS/2 System window has been moved.

You can vary an OS/2 window's height and width by manipulating the *size* widget. The size widget, indicated in Figure 1-5, is the entire border that encloses the window. When you move the mouse pointer on top of the border, it changes shape to a double arrowhead.

When the pointer assumes the double arrowhead shape on the bottom border, you can enlarge the window by dragging the bottom border down or shrink it by dragging the bottom border up. The same thing happens when you place the pointer on the left, right and top borders. With this technique, window-size changes are restricted to one dimension.

You can change a window's size in two dimensions simultaneously by placing the mouse pointer on one of the window's four corners. The double arrowhead that appears is inclined at a 45-degree angle from the vertical. When you drag the lower right corner of the window further to the right and down, the window enlarges in both directions.

With the size widget you can make a window as big or small as you want (within limits). You can make it wide or narrow, tall or short.

Make your windows just large enough to display the objects they contain. That way you will not unnecessarily obscure other windows or objects on the desktop. Generally, OS/2's default window sizes waste considerable space. By downsizing these windows you can show more of your desktop. Figure 1-7 shows the desktop after the OS/2 System window shown in Figure 1-5 has been resized to conserve space. It has also been rearranged by selecting Arrange from its System menu after the resizing operation was completed.

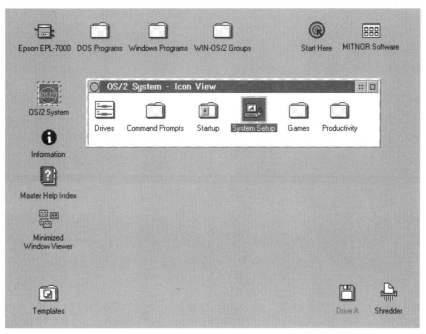

Figure 1-7: OS/2 System window has been resized.

There are many occasions when you may want to focus on one application to the exclusion of all others. In those cases, having windows on the screen showing other applications is more of a distraction than a help. Furthermore, it limits the amount you can see in the client area of the application of primary interest.

Maximize a window when you want to concentrate on it fully.
The *maximize* widget is located in the upper right corner of
every window. It is square shaped and has an open square symbol
inside it (see Figure 1-5). When you click on this widget, its window
expands to fill the entire screen. Figure 1-8 shows the effect of maxi-
mizing the OS/2 System window.

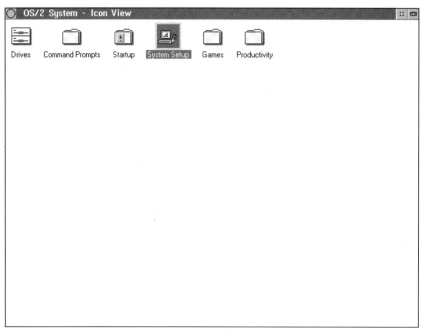

Figure 1-8: Maximized OS/2 System window.

**Return a maximized window to its normal size when you are
finished with it.** Notice that the upper right corner of a maximized window contains a different symbol, a small square with
vertical lines on left and right. This is the *restore* widget. When you
click on it the maximized window is restored to its original size.

Minimize active windows to unclutter the desktop. Immediately
to the left of either the maximize or restore widget (whichever
applies) in the upper-right corner of a window, is the *minimize*
widget. It has a square shape and contains a square symbol that is
smaller than the maximize widget's square symbol. When you click

on the minimize widget, its window disappears completely from the desktop. This does not close the application, however. It is still running, although not visible. You can restore a minimized window to the desktop by pressing Ctrl-Esc. This pops up a window named Window List (Figure 1-9).

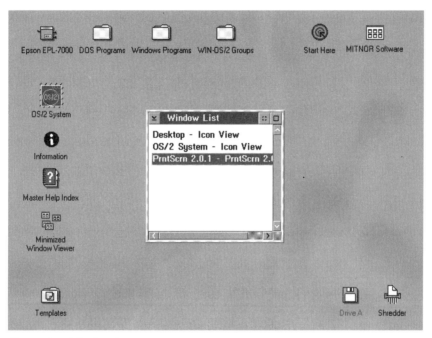

Figure 1-9: Window List.

The Window List displays a list of all the sessions that are currently running. In Figure 1-9 we see that the Desktop window is running, as it almost always is when OS/2 is running. The OS/2 System window is also running, although it has been minimized and thus is not visible. Finally, an application named PrntScrn 2.0.1 is running. PrntScrn is the program used to capture the screen images in this book. It is also minimized so it can perform its screen capture function without drawing undue attention to itself. Double-clicking on the session you want to work with gives it the focus by making it the active window.

The Minimized Windows Viewer is another tool for displaying which applications are running minimized or "in the background." In Figure 1-5 its icon is located at the lower-left portion of the desktop. Double-clicking on the icon displays the Minimized Window Viewer shown in Figure 1-10.

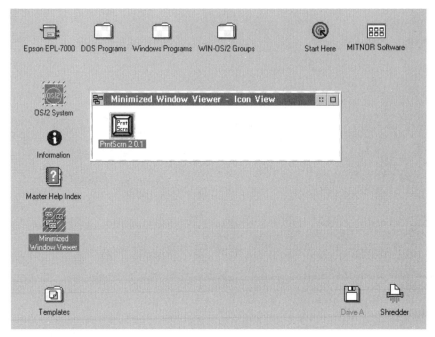

Figure 1-10: Minimized Window Viewer window.

The PrntScrn icon is displayed, but no icon is seen for the Desktop folder or the OS/2 System folder. The Minimized Window Viewer displays the icons of running applications but not of other objects, such as folders.

 To give a minimized application the focus, just double-click on its icon in the Minimized Window Viewer.

Active applications can be minimized to the desktop. If you prefer this method (as in Windows 3.1) over using the Minimized Window Viewer, you can change the default behavior by selecting System Setup from the OS/2 System folder. First select System from the System Setup folder. In the notebook that appears, select the Window tab, then click on the "Minimize window to desktop" radio button. The minimization behavior will be changed from now on.

There is good reason to continue to keep the icons of minimized applications in the Viewer folder. Since OS/2 is a more powerful system than Windows, you probably will have more applications running, but minimized, than is typical for Windows. To keep the desktop from becoming cluttered with icons, it is convenient to store them in the Minimized Icon Viewer.

If you see scroll bars, this is a signal that there is more to the window than meets the eye. Often a window's client area is not big enough to display everything that it should. You can view the unseen parts of the object by scrolling the display. Figure 1-11 shows scroll bars on the right and lower borders of a resized OS/2 System window. There is a *slider* in the vertical scroll bar, indicating that something is hidden below the window. The horizontal scroll bar's slider is long and is positioned to the left of the window indicating that something (but not much) is off-screen to the right. A shorter scroll bar would mean that there was more material off-screen.

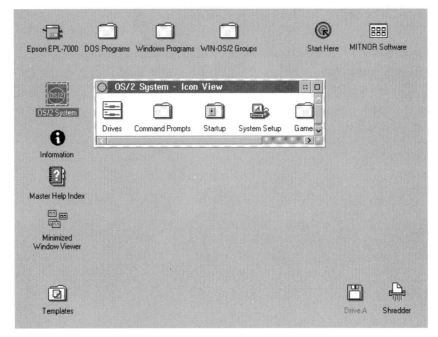

Figure 1-11: Resized OS/2 System window.

By placing the mouse pointer on the horizontal slider and sliding it to the right, you can display the hidden material. At the same time, the left most information has now scrolled off the left edge of the window (Figure 1-12). You can also scroll the display by clicking on the arrowheads at either end of the scroll bar.

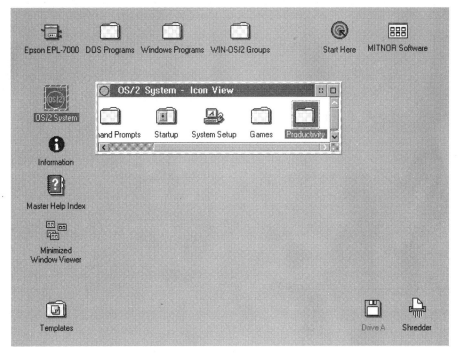

Figure 1-12: OS/2 System window has been scrolled to the right.

An alternative to scrolling the Window List window would be to resize it to make it bigger. If you did that, scrolling would not be necessary. Clearly, as shown in Figures 1-11 and 1-12, resizing is the better choice. Sometimes, however, the area to be displayed is larger than the entire display screen. In those instances, scrolling is the best way to make sure you see everything.

Close all windows containing objects (clients) that you will not be using again soon. As long as a window is open it is consuming memory. Since people always want their computer to do more things and to do them faster, system memory is a precious commodity. When you close a window, its memory allocation is returned to OS/2, making it available to other processes. You close a window by double-clicking on its close icon, which is a square located in the upper left corner of the window. The close widget contains a small icon, which varies depending on the window's underlying function. For the OS/2 System window it is an open circle. When you close a window, it disappears from the desktop, and its name is removed from the Window List.

MENU MAGIC

Although the OS/2 Workplace Shell is more icon-oriented than the Microsoft Windows desktop, you can also use pop-up windows to communicate with it in much the same way that the Microsoft product uses pull-down menus. Many menu options invoke functions that you can also perform with icon manipulations or by pressing the appropriate function keys. Some functions can be performed only from the menus.

Every window has at least one menu associated with it, the System menu. The contents of a window's System menu vary, depending on the nature of the client it holds. Some such menus have many options. Others have only a few.

You can display a window's System menu by clicking either mouse button on the square widget in the upper left corner of the window. Earlier we called this widget the Close widget, because when you double-click button 1 on it, the window is closed. It serves a double purpose. Single-clicking with either button 1 or button 2 displays the System menu, so it is also referred to as the System Menu widget. Figure 1-13 shows the System menu for the OS/2 System window.

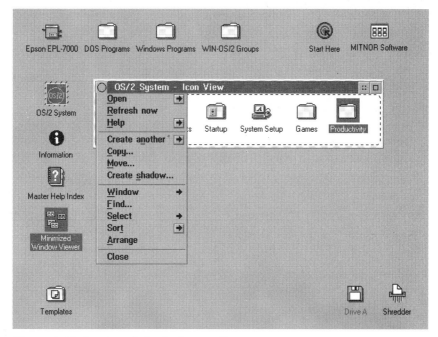

Figure 1-13: System window's System Menu.

Follow the arrows to submenus. Arrows to the right of the Open, Help, Create another, Window, Select and Sort options indicate that they lead to submenus. Clicking button 1 on the arrow will display the associated submenu. Figure 1-14 shows the System menu with the Window submenu pulled down.

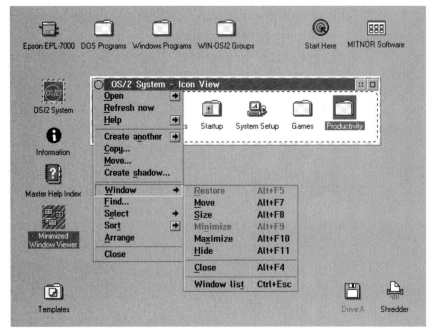

Figure 1-14: Cascading menus.

Options on the menu duplicate functions that can be performed by manipulating widgets. To the right of each option is listed a function key combination that will perform the same operation. So, for example, there are three separate and distinct ways of closing a window.

Some options on a window's System menu determine which of several modes of operation are in effect. Figure 1-15 shows one such case, where the Open option on the OS/2 System window's System menu has been selected, displaying a submenu with several choices. There is a check mark beside the Icon view option, showing that it is active and the Tree view and Details view are not.

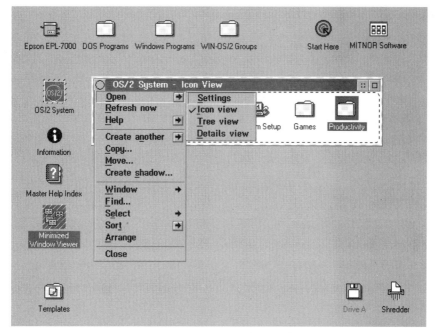

Figure 1-15: A submenu shows several modes of operation.

It is easy to cancel a menu selection. If you have made a series of selections from a family of cascaded menus, you can cancel everything with a single action. Simply click mouse button 1 outside the window, or press Ctrl-\.

Dimmed menu choices are unavailable. Sometimes a menu option will be "grayed out" as the Restore and Minimize options are in the Window submenu in Figure 1-14. Options that have been grayed out may not be selected at present. For example, since the OS/2 System window in Figure 1-14 is already normal size, it does not make sense to Restore it to normal size again. It may, however, be Moved, Sized, Maximized, Hidden or Closed.

DIALOG BOXES

A *dialog box* is a specialized window that serves a particular purpose. As its name implies, it is used to exchange information between OS/2 and the user. Users may read information in the box, then respond to it by making mouse selections or by entering text into fields provided for that purpose.

Dialog boxes generally pop up when OS/2 or an application running under it needs some information from the user. They are similar to other windows in that they have a title bar and are movable, but they cannot be resized or scrolled. They can, however, contain fields (called *list boxes*) that can be scrolled.

Dialog boxes usually appear when you make a selection from a menu. If the option chosen requires additional information before it can perform its function, it displays a dialog box. Figure 1-16 shows the dialog box that appears when you select Open from the OS/2 System Editor File menu.

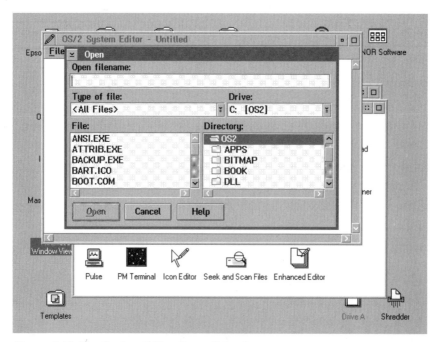

Figure 1-16: The System Editor Open dialog box.

The dialog box in Figure 1-16 is asking for the name of the file to open. You can enter the name directly into the data entry field labeled "Open filename:" or home in on the file by selecting from list boxes the type of file, the drive, the directory, and finally, its filename.

 If you are not exactly sure of the spelling of a file name but would recognize it in a list, use the list box method of file selection. In addition to their title bar, system menu and data entry fields, dialog boxes have list boxes and buttons. As we have seen, list boxes can display a list of choices from which the user makes selections. Various types of buttons are available for making different kinds of selections.

Pushbutton

The pushbutton is the most common dialog box control. It's a rectangle with a shaded border, rounded corners and a text label in its center.

 When you click button 1 on a pushbutton, the application running in the window immediately performs the function indicated by the button label. In Figure 1-16 there are three pushbuttons labeled Open, Cancel and Help. The Open button is currently grayed out, indicating that its function is not available. Once a filename has been entered into the filename field, the pushbutton will become fully visible, indicating that a file can be opened.

Radio Button

Radio buttons are named after the buttons you push on a car radio to select a station. Only one station can be selected at a time, so when you push the button in for a new radio station, the button for the station you were listening to pops out.

In OS/2, radio buttons are used when you want to make a group of selections mutually exclusive. Only one button in the set may be selected at any one time. Figure 1-17 shows the first page of the OS/2 System folder Settings notebook (to be discussed in detail in Chapter 2, "Personalizing Your Desktop"). The figure shows radio buttons in the Format and Icon display areas. Currently, Non-grid is selected in the Format area and Normal size is selected in the Icon display area. If you click on either Flowed or Non-flowed, the black dot in the Non-grid button will disappear then reappear in the button you selected. The same thing would happen in the Icon display area if you selected Small size.

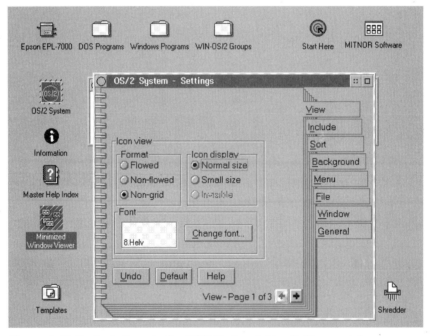

Figure 1-17: Radio buttons in the OS/2 System folder Settings notebook.

Check Box

Like radio buttons, check boxes usually appear in groups. But unlike radio buttons, they do not denote mutually exclusive choices. Figure 1-18 shows the System Configuration dialog box, accessible from the Selective Install choice under the System Setup icon in the OS/2 System window. In the Currently Installed Peripherals group, both

SCSI Adapter Support and Printer have been checked. Both of these settings will be changed to new values during the current session.

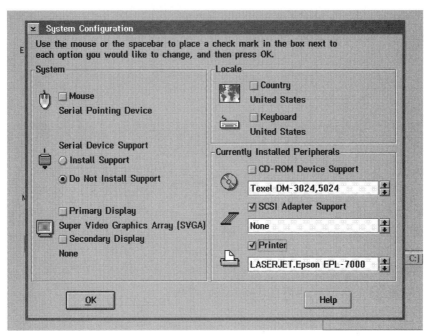

Figure 1-18: The System Configuration dialog box, showing check boxes.

Spin Button

Use a spin button to select one value from a list. A window displays the current value and nearby arrowheads allow you to either increment or decrement it to the desired value. When you click on one of the arrows with mouse button 1, values spin by like the numbers on an automobile odometer. Figure 1-19 shows the Autosave dialog box, accessible from the File menu of the OS/2 System Editor.

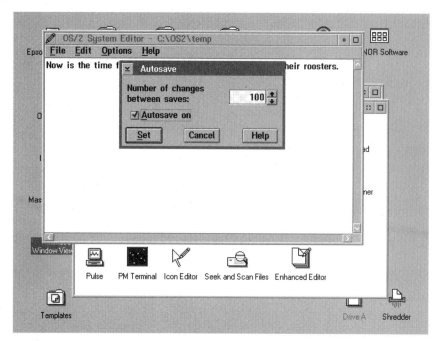

Figure 1-19: Spin button in Autosave dialog box.

Slider Box

Slider boxes are analogous to the controls on equalizers and other audio equipment. Drag sliders to the desired position with your mouse. Figure 1-20 shows the Timing page of the Mouse-Settings notebook that is in the System Setup folder. The sliders control the interval between clicks that OS/2 will interpret as a double click and the speed with which the mouse pointer on the screen will track the movement of the mouse.

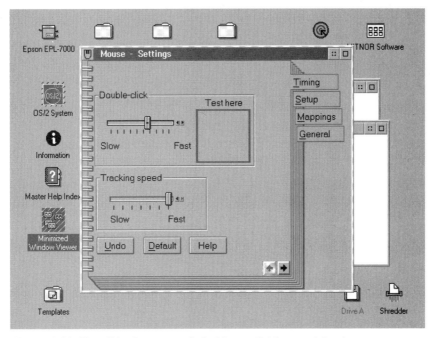

Figure 1-20: The slider box controls in Mouse-Settings notebook.

ALTERNATE USER INTERFACES

In addition to the desktop, OS/2 offers three other user interfaces, each of which has an advantage when running certain kinds of applications.

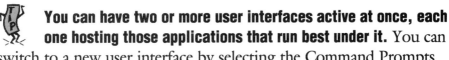 **You can have two or more user interfaces active at once, each one hosting those applications that run best under it.** You can switch to a new user interface by selecting the Command Prompts folder from the OS/2 System window (Figure 1-21).

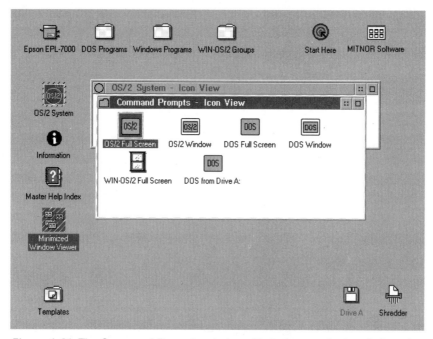

Figure 1-21: The Command Prompts window. Six icons are displayed, three for DOS interfaces, one for a WIN-OS/2 interface and two for OS/2 interfaces.

DOS Interfaces

You can run one or more DOS sessions under OS/2. These sessions are not real DOS but an emulation that allows you to run the large majority of DOS programs under OS/2.

A few programs may not run in an OS/2 DOS session. These are mainly programs that manipulate the hardware directly rather than going through DOS (disk utilities, virus detection programs, games). Nearly everything else will run without problems.

If you want to give the entire screen to the DOS application you are starting, select DOS Full Screen from the Command Prompts window. A DOS command prompt similar to that displayed by real DOS will be displayed, waiting for you to enter a DOS command or program name.

Select DOS Window if you want to start a DOS session in a window. You could actually start and monitor several windowed DOS sessions on the screen at the same time.

 To switch back from a DOS full-screen session to the OS/2 desktop, press Ctrl-Esc.

To end a DOS session, type EXIT at the DOS prompt.

You can boot and use real DOS, while OS/2 remains resident in memory. The third DOS interface, DOS from Drive A:, allows for the starting of real DOS, not an emulation. You might use this if the application you want to run requires a particular version of DOS that differs from OS/2's emulation. Place a DOS boot disk into drive A before selecting this icon. OS/2 will initiate the booting of DOS from the floppy. You can then proceed to run applications that require real DOS. When you are finished you can return to OS/2 by pressing Ctrl-Esc. OS/2 has been waiting patiently in the background for you to finish with DOS and return to the OS/2 desktop.

Although booting a DOS floppy from within OS/2 creates an environment very close to that when DOS completely controls the hardware, it is not identical. Some programs, such as some games that are heavily graphical, may not run in this mode, although they do run if DOS is booted up from scratch using the same boot floppy.

Although pressing Ctrl-Esc gets you back from real DOS to the OS/2 desktop, the DOS session is still active. If you shut down the system now, OS/2 will remember that DOS from Drive A: was active. The next time you bring OS/2 up, it will insist that your DOS boot disk be installed in drive A. Typing EXIT at the DOS prompt will *not* terminate the session, because real DOS does not recognize the EXIT command. To end a real DOS session, first press Alt-Home. This will display the desktop with a DOS window on it. Open the window's System menu by clicking button 1 or by pressing Alt again, then select Close from the menu that drops down. This will close the real DOS session and allow you to run once again without a DOS boot disk in drive A.

WIN-OS/2

WIN-OS/2 is OS/2's emulation of Microsoft Windows 3.1. With it you can host any well-behaved Windows 3.1 application. The WIN-OS/2 desktop, shown in Figure 1-22, looks very much like a standard Windows 3.1 desktop. In the lower left corner of the screen is the OS/2 Desktop icon. Double clicking on the OS/2 Desktop icon returns you to the OS/2 desktop, while leaving the WIN-OS2 session active but minimized.

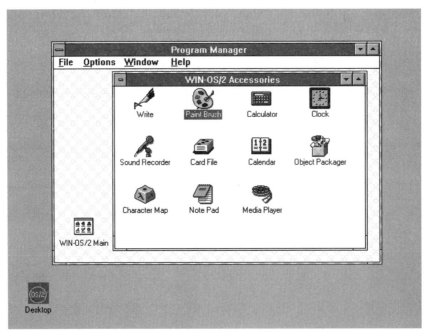

Figure 1-22: The WIN-OS/2 desktop.

 You may install Windows applications under WIN-OS2 in exactly the same manner that you would install them under Windows 3.1. They should operate identically, except that under OS/2 2.1 you can have several instances of WIN-OS2 operating simultaneously. DOS allows only one copy of real Windows 3.1 active at a time.

OS/2 Shell

Two OS/2 icons are displayed in the Command Prompts window in
Figure 1-21, OS/2 Full Screen and OS/2 Window. Selecting one of
these will display the OS/2 command prompt interface. The Full
Screen selection will display a non-graphical, character-oriented
screen with a Help line at the top and the OS/2 command prompt
just below it. The OS/2 Window selection will show the same thing,
but it will be contained in a window on the OS/2 desktop rather than
monopolizing the whole screen (Figure 1-23).

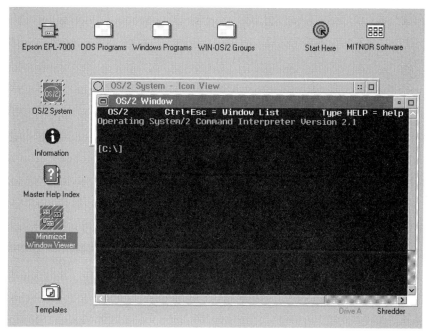

Figure 1-23: OS/2 Window command prompt.

**At the OS/2 prompt you can directly enter commands in the OS/2
command language, which overlaps considerably with the DOS
batch language.** A few DOS batch commands do not carry over to
OS/2, and a few OS/2 commands do not function under DOS.

Switch environments quickly with Ctrl-Esc. Regardless of which user interface is currently on the screen, when you press Ctrl-Esc the Workplace Shell appears with the Window list displayed. From it you can select any active window or full screen process by double-clicking on it. This is the fastest way to move from one OS/2 application to another, from one Windows application to another, or across systems among DOS, Windows and OS/2.

WHEN ALL ELSE FAILS, CLICK ON HELP

There are a few fundamental things a newcomer to OS/2 should learn in order to stay out of trouble. First and foremost is how to get help when you feel you ought to be able to perform a function but don't know how to do it.

Everyone remembers the pearl of ancient wisdom that says, "When all else fails, read the directions." Usually the "directions" come in the form of printed manuals delivered with a software product. OS/2 comes with remarkably little in manuals and printed matter of other kinds. This is fine, since most people either ignore or quickly lose such manuals. OS/2 comes equipped with extensive on-line help. Since it is right there on your hard disk, you cannot lose it. It is never more than a few keystrokes away. Generally, when you are attempting to perform a particular function, there is context sensitive help available. You can select Help from the menu bar of the window you are working in. Sometimes, however, you may not even know where to start. In those cases, you may want to double-click on one of three icons that appear on the desktop when it is first installed.

When you don't know what to do next, activate one of the three Help icons on the desktop. The three icons are named "Start Here," "Information" and "Master Help Index."

Start Here

When you double-click on the Start Here icon, a dialog box is displayed that contains two windows (Figure 1-24). The window on the left shows contents of the major topics covered.

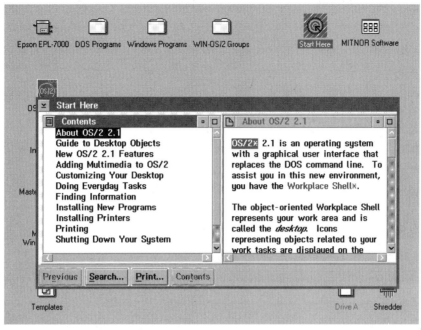

Figure 1-24: The Start Here dialog box.

Select one of the choices in the left window to display help text corresponding to that choice in the right window. The help file displayed in the right window is structured as *hypertext*. Key words within the displayed text are displayed in a different color and are also indicated by an asterisk. Double-clicking on these words displays more detailed help on them. Help text is sometimes supplemented by graphics.

At the bottom of the Start Here dialog box are four push buttons labeled Previous, Search, Print and Index. When you click on the Previous button, it causes the display in the right window to revert to its appearance before the most recent change. Thus if you had been looking at help text, then double-clicked on a key word to display more detail on it, pressing Previous would redisplay the original help text. Press the Search button to display a dialog box allowing you to enter a word or phrase that might appear in the help file. You can restrict the search to selected areas or search the entire help file. The Print button allows you to print out some or all of the on-line help text. The Index button redisplays the table of contents in the left window, in case that window had been prematurely closed.

Information

Double-clicking the Information icon displays a window containing several categories of help (Figure 1-25).

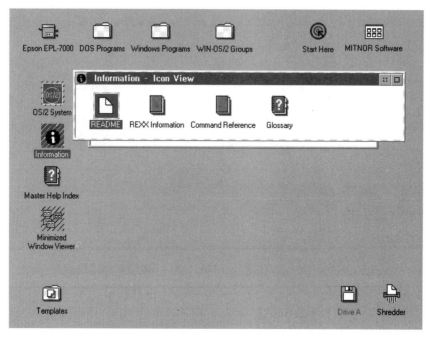

Figure 1-25: Information window.

One of the first things you should do after starting to use OS/2 is to double-click on the README icon. Read the latest information about your version of OS/2 that was discovered too late to be included in the printed documentation or regular on-line help. You can often save yourself hours of frustration by studying the information in README before you try to figure out why OS/2 is not working the way you think it should.

REXX Information gives detailed information about the REXX script language, used to write programs to run under OS/2. It gives programmers considerably more power than a batch language, but without the complexity of a full development language such as C.

Command Reference describes the OS/2 command or batch language, giving full descriptions and syntax for all commands. The Tutorial walks the user through very basic information about using OS/2. The Glossary gives definitions for words as OS/2 uses them. These definitions themselves may contain keywords whose definitions can in turn be displayed by double-clicking.

Master Help Index

The Master Help Index contains over 5,000 entries, each one pointing to specific help text. As is the case with Start Here, when you double-click on the Master Help Index icon, a pair of windows appears. The index is on the left and the help text for the currently selected entry is on the right. Previous, Search, Print and Index pushbuttons give you the power to navigate through the material quickly and easily to obtain the information you want.

Application Help

In addition to the general help available from the desktop, each OS/2 application has help that has been provided by its developers. Most applications have a Help option on their menu bar. When you select it, a menu drops down from which you can select a specific kind of help. Your selection will open a help window, either containing or pointing to the information you seek. Figure 1-26 shows the Help window for the OS/2 System Editor. Structurally it is consistent with the desktop help tools we have seen. Help facilities for other applications are similar.

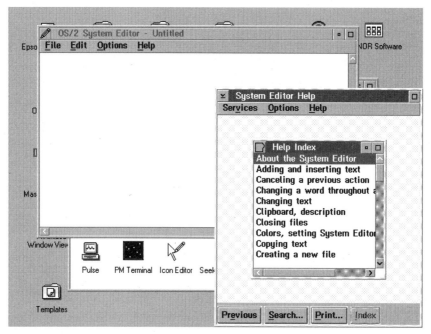

Figure 1-26: An application specific help window.

MOVING ON

You now have the basic tools that will allow you to operate with OS/2. With their default settings, they do a fine job in most situations. The next chapter will tell you how to shape those tools to make OS/2 look the way you want it to look and act the way you want it to act.

Chapter 2

PERSONALIZING YOUR DESKTOP

OS/2's Workplace Shell not only gives you a friendly graphical user interface, but allows you to modify many aspects of it to match your own personal preferences. Some power users want a lean and mean interface that places a minimum of performance-robbing interaction between the user and the hardware. Others want all the help they can get and look to the operating system to provide it. Some want hair-trigger responsiveness to keyboard or mouse input. Others do not want the computer to accept a character until they have held a key down for a good long time. Some people prefer a screen made up of soothing pastel shades, while others prefer the alertness-inducing properties of bright neon colors. OS/2 accommodates all these requirements plus quite a few others.

You can customize many of OS/2's features from the System Setup folder in the OS/2 System Window. Figure 2-1 shows the desktop with the System Setup folder opened. You can control much of the look, feel and behavior of OS/2 from here.

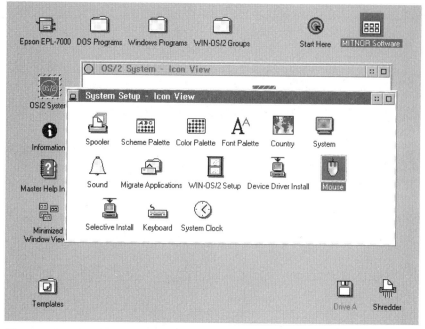

Figure 2-1: The System Setup folder.

TEACH YOUR OLD MOUSE NEW TRICKS

In a GUI-based system such as OS/2, much of your interaction with the computer is done through the mouse. It is important to customize the mouse to your preferences. You can adjust the way the mouse responds to your hand movements. You can program the buttons so they are optimized for either a right-handed (the default) or left-handed user. You can even program the buttons to perform operations not normally performed by a mouse.

Changing the Mouse Double-Click Interval & Tracking Speed

OS/2 follows the convention that clicking once on an object's icon will select the object, and clicking twice will activate it. OS/2 must be able to discriminate between an activating double-click and two single clicks that were meant to select but not activate the object.

You can specify your preferred double-click interval, as well as other mouse features, by selecting System Setup from the System Menu, then double-clicking on the Mouse icon displayed in the

System Setup window. The Mouse Settings notebook (Figure 2-2) is displayed on the screen.

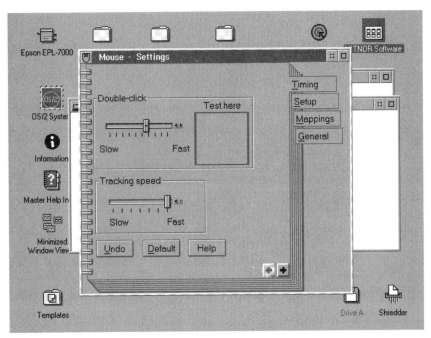

Figure 2-2: The Mouse Settings notebook, showing the Timing page.

The notebook has four pages, with tabs labeled Timing, Setup, Mappings and General. On the Timing page, you can specify the double-click interval and the speed with which the pointer on the screen tracks the motion of the mouse on your mouse pad. The double-click slider box shows that the current setting is a little faster than midway between the slowest and the fastest settings.

By moving the slider with the mouse, you can make the double-click interval longer or shorter. The "Test here" box gives you a place to experiment until you find your optimal setting.

The tracking speed slider alters the speed with which the pointer on the screen follows the motion of the mouse. When the speed is Fast, as in Figure 2-2, a relatively small movement of the mouse produces a large movement of the pointer. When the tracking speed is set to Slow, a large mouse movement causes a relatively small pointer movement.

The mouse settings in Figure 2-2 are the default settings. For most people they are fine. If these settings are ever changed, you can easily return to the default settings by clicking on the Default button at the bottom of the notebook page.

It's Done With Mirrors—Left-Handed Mousing

In many applications, mouse movements are used to make very fine adjustments. Since most people have more control over small, precise movements with their dominant hand, it makes sense to set the mouse up to be used by that hand. Most people are right-handed, so mouse software is generally written so that the most frequently used mouse button (button 1) is under the index finger of the right hand. This is great for right-handers, but less than swell for lefties like me. OS/2 accommodates southpaws by offering a mouse setting that reverses the identities of button 1 and button 2. A left-hander can manipulate such a mirror-image mouse with all the skill that a right-hander displays with the default settings.

For a left-handed mouse, click on the notebook's Setup tab. A right-handed and a left-handed illustration are shown, with a box around the currently selected alternative (Figure 2-3). Click on the one you want and the operation of the mouse will immediately be changed to reflect your selection.

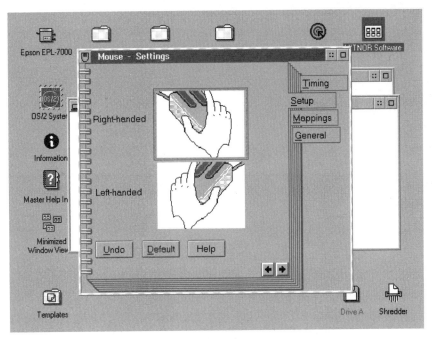

Figure 2-3: The Mouse Settings notebook Setup page.

Mapping Functions to Control Key/Mouse Button Combinations

You don't need voodoo to figure out the two most common uses of
the buttons on your mouse. They are the same as what you find on
Microsoft Windows and the Macintosh System 7 operating system.
When you click button 1, you are selecting the object under the
pointer. When you double-click button 1, you are opening or activating the object under the pointer. However, the mouse buttons,
particularly when pressed in conjunction with one or more keys on
the keyboard, can do much more for you. Table 2-1 lists additional
functions you can perform with mouse clicks and with mouse click/
key combinations.

Table 2-1. Standard functions performed with mouse clicks.

Function	Click/key Combination
Select object	Click mouse button 1 on object
Open object	Double-click button 1 on object
Display window list	Click both buttons on desktop
Display object pop-up menu	Click button 2 on object
Drag (move) an object	Move mouse while pressing button 2
Copy an object	Move mouse while pressing Ctrl and button 2
Create a shadow object	Move mouse while pressing Ctrl, Shift and button 2
Select adjacent objects	Press Shift while clicking button 1 on each object
Select nonadjacent objects	Press Ctrl while clicking button 1 on each object
Change an object's name	Press Alt while clicking button 1 on the object

KEYBOARD CUSTOMIZATION

The keyboard is the user's primary input device for communicating with OS/2. Many common input operations have been assigned keys or combinations of keys. In most cases, these operations duplicate what can be accomplished with the mouse.

Default Keystroke Assignments

Quite a few keys and key combinations have been assigned desktop control functions. In most cases you would not want to change any of these assignments. Table 2-2 enumerates the most common keyboard controls. Some of these functions are context sensitive. They vary depending upon what you are doing.

Table 2-2. Standard functions performed by key depression.

Function	Keystroke
Toggle the window menu or object menu	Alt
Switch to the next open object	Alt+Esc
Close the active object or window	Alt+F4
Restore window to original size	Alt+F5
Switch between object and its help window	Alt+F6
Switch between entry and Master Help Index	Alt+F6
Move the window	Alt+F7, Arrow keys
Size the window	Alt+F8, Arrow keys
Minimize the window	Alt+F9
Maximize the window	Alt+F10
Hide a window	Alt+F11
Move from notebook tab to notebook page	Alt+Down arrow
Move from notebook page to notebook tab	Alt+Up arrow
Move to next notebook page	Alt+Page Down
Move to previous notebook page	Alt+Page Up
Set window default size	Alt,S,Arrows, Enter
Switch focus to the desktop	Alt+Shift+Tab
Display pop-up menu for a window	Alt+Spacebar
Switch to next open window on desktop	Alt+Tab
Move among objects	Arrows
Restart the system	Ctrl+Alt+Del
Display the Window List	Ctrl+Esc
Scroll window to right	Ctrl+Page Down
Scroll window to left	Ctrl+Page Up
Search for word or phrase in help window	Ctrl+S

Function	Keystroke
Select all objects	Ctrl+/
Deselect all objects	Ctrl+\
Select the bottom right window object	End
Select a pop-up menu's last choice	End
Open the selected object	Enter
In Help, select previous help window	Esc
Get Help	F1
Display General help in Help Window	F2
Display Keys help in Help Window	F9
Move to and from the menu bar	F10
Display Help index in Help Window	F11
Select the top left window object	Home
Select the pop-up menu's first choice	Home
Move down through window one page at a time	Page Down
Move up through window one page at a time	Page Up
Select multiple objects (Add mode toggle)	Shift+F8
Display pop-up menu	Shift+F10
Select or deselect an object	Spacebar
Move to the next Notebook field	Tab
Move to Master Help Index related information	Tab

You can reassign some of the key combinations that produce desktop actions if you have a good reason to do so. Always be aware, however, that you may be introducing a possible confusion factor whenever you move away from the default assignments.

In an imperfect world such as ours, hardware (as well as software) sometimes fails. The mouse pointer may refuse to follow the moves you make with the mouse. The screen may become corrupted so you cannot see where to click to perform a desired function (such as exiting a renegade application). It is comforting to know you can perform these same functions from the keyboard, regardless of the location of the pointer.

If you make a selection that OS/2 cannot cope with, causing your pointer to turn into a clock face and stay that way, press Alt+F4 to back out of the problem.

Making Custom Key Assignments

Of all the functions listed in Table 2-2, OS/2 allows you to change the keys that invoke two of them: displaying pop-up menus and editing title text. The Keyboard Settings notebook, accessible from the System Setup window, has a Mappings tab.

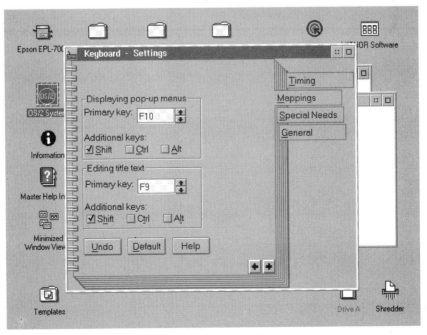

Figure 2-4: The Mappings page of Keyboard Settings notebook.

As you can see in Figure 2-4, the default setting for displaying pop-up menus is Shift+F10 and the default setting for editing title text is Shift+F9. You can change Shift to Ctrl, Alt, or no additional key, and you can select any function key as well as Insert, Delete, Home, End, Page Up, Page Down or Enter.

Display pop-up menus with a single keystroke. Since this is something you will probably do fairly often, you might want to replace the default two-key combination with, say, F12.

Choose Your Own Keyboard Rates

Aside from reassigning keys, OS/2 offers additional ways to customize the keyboard. You can alter the way it responds to the pressing of a key and the way it displays the cursor on the screen.

The Keyboard Settings notebook has a Timing page similar to that in the Mouse Settings notebook. From here you can control the keyboard repeat rate, the repeat delay rate and the cursor blink rate. Figure 2-5 shows that each of these rates is controlled by a slider.

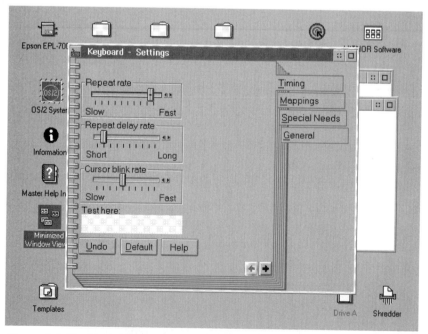

Figure 2-5: The Timing page of Keyboard Settings notebook.

The repeat rate and repeat delay rate control behavior when the user presses a key and keeps holding it down. When a key is held down, the character it represents is repeatedly sent to the screen. The repeat rate determines the interval between when two characters are sent. The repeat delay rate determines the interval between when the key is first pressed and when the first character in the repeat sequence is sent. The cursor blink rate controls the visual appearance of the cursor on the screen.

If you are the only one using a computer, set the repeat rate, repeat delay rate and cursor blink rate to the values that are most comfortable for you. If you share the machine with someone else, either come to a consensus on rates or leave them at the default values. Most people never change the default values because they don't know they can.

PERSONALIZE SYSTEM OBJECT ICONS

The OS/2 desktop, like all modern graphical user interfaces, makes heavy use of icons. An icon is a small picture that reminds the user of the function of the underlying object. IBM supplies icons for all OS/2 system objects and third-party application vendors provide icons for their products. Users can change these icons if they wish, or even create new icons from scratch. OS/2's tool for icon creation and modification is the Icon Editor, which is in the Productivity folder contained in the System folder.

Most of the icons included in OS/2 can be modified or replaced with icons that you create with the Icon Editor. Third-party applications, however, often have copyrighted icons which are not susceptible to modification or replacement. Of course you may create any icons you wish for your own applications. Chapter 7, "Productivity Programs," gives you detailed instructions for creating a new icon.

FOLDER SETTINGS

The first time a folder expands into a window on the desktop, it exhibits the system default appearance and behavior. The appearance is "plain vanilla" and the behavior is pretty much what you would expect. You can change both to fit your preferences, your moods or your fancies.

The tools for making these changes are in each folder's Settings notebook which you can access by clicking button 2 on the folder's icon on the desktop. The System notebook appears, displaying eight tabbed sections. The View section is on top.

View Tab

There are three pages in the View section, each corresponding to one of the three ways folder objects can be displayed: icon view, tree view or details view. In icon view you may alter the way the icons are displayed, their size and the font used in the icon name. In tree view you can specify whether lines connect the folder with nested subfolders or other objects, as well as icon size and font. In details view you can select the type of object to be displayed, display selected information about those objects and specify display font.

 The Undo button at the bottom of each page returns settings to their condition at the start of the session.

 The Default button returns settings to their default values.

Include Tab

With the Include tab, you can specify which objects in a folder are displayed and which are not. The default situation is to include all objects. You can selectively exclude those you don't want to show. Figure 2-6 shows the first page of the Include section of the Settings notebook. All objects, regardless of name and regardless of type, are selected.

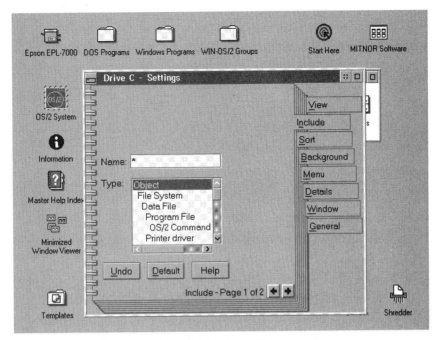

Figure 2-6: The Settings notebook Include section, page 1.

When these default settings are applied to the display of the root directory of drive C, the window shown in Figure 2-7 results. The desktop folder is shown, along with a number of others. The AUTOEXEC.BAT and CONFIG.SYS files are present as are miscellaneous drivers, backups and other junk. Conspicuous in their absence are hidden files. There are bound to be some in the root directory of the boot disk, but they do not show up in the default display.

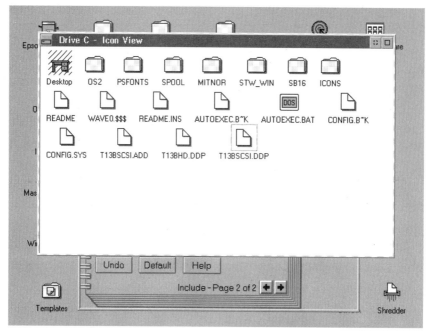

Figure 2-7: The Drive C folder with default Include settings.

You can display hidden files, without having to know in advance what their names are, or change their file attributes. This is done from page 2 of the Include section of Drive C's Settings notebook (Figure 2-6).

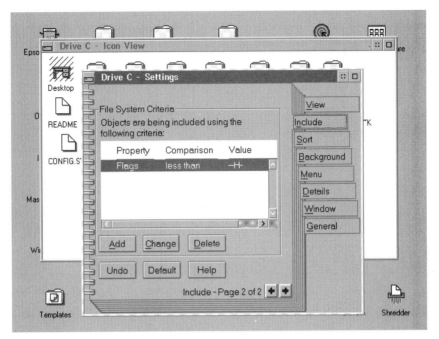

Figure 2-8: Page 2 of Include section.

Objects are included in the display if their flags have a value of less than -H-. H is the hidden flag, so hidden files are explicitly excluded by this criterion. We can include them by clicking on the Change button and modifying the change criteria in the dialog box that pops up. To include hidden files change the comparison type to "greater or equal" and change the "H" to a "-".

Now when you look at the Drive C Icon View, a number of files have been added to the display (Figure 2-9). They have names such as EA DATA. SF, WP ROOT. SF, OS2KRNL, OS2LDR, OS2VER, OS2BOOT, OS2LDR.MSG and OS2DUMP.

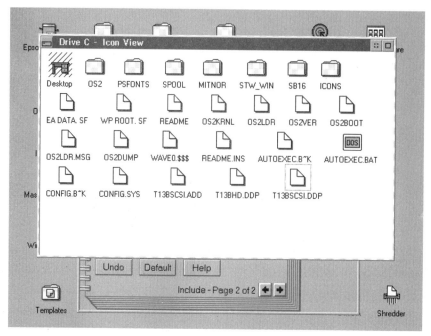

Figure 2-9: The Drives folder showing hidden files.

If you want to display only executable files, select a Type of
Program File from page 1 of the Include section, deselecting the
Type Object at the same time. (Refer to Figure 2-6.) Display of
everything except AUTOEXEC.BAT and CONFIG.SYS is now
suppressed (Figure 2-10).

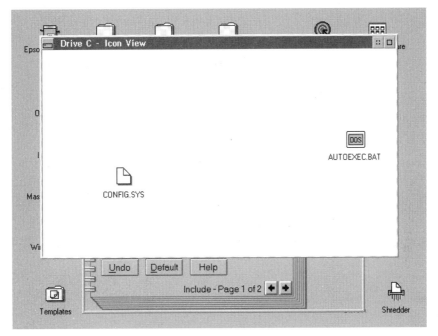

Figure 2-10: Only executable files are displayed.

Sort Tab, Background Tab, Menu Tab & Window Tab

The Sort tab allows you to change the criteria used to sort the display of objects in a window. The default is to sort by object name. If two names are the same, a series of secondary sort keys come into play until a difference is finally found. You can change the primary sort key and any or all of the secondary sort keys.

With the Background tab you can choose a new background color for a window or replace the solid color with a bitmapped image. A number of such bitmaps are supplied with OS/2, or you can use a bitmap of your own design.

Bitmapped images can be very pretty but are usually not a good idea for backgrounds. Patterns in the image may make it difficult to see the objects that are arrayed in front. In addition, bitmapped images take up considerable memory. Your system will be able to support more open windows and will redraw the screen faster if all your window backgrounds are a solid color.

You can add additional menu actions to the desktop pop-up menu or any other window's menu, using that window's Settings notebook Menu tab. From the menu options you add, you can append cascaded submenus. Each menu option would stand for a program that would execute when the option is selected.

The Window tab controls how windows are opened and minimized. If a window is already open and you click on its icon again, the default setting causes OS/2 to change the focus to the existing window. You can change this behavior so that instead of returning to the existing window, another instance of the window is created.

The default action for minimization is to place the icon of the minimized object into the Minimized Icon Viewer. You may choose to minimize the object to the desktop instead, or to hide the minimized object completely. If you choose to hide it, it will still be shown in the Window List, and you can activate it from there.

File Tab

Files as well as folders have a File tab in their Settings notebook. The section under the File tab has three pages, the second of which is the most interesting. With it you can see the date the file or folder was last changed as well as its size and the size of its extended attributes. You can also change the object's Read-only, Archive, Hidden and System attributes. If you check the box for a file's Read-only attribute, the file can no longer be changed or deleted. If you check the Hidden attribute, it will no longer show up in directories displayed from the OS/2 command prompt, nor will its icon appear in its folder's window. The Archive flag indicates whether the file has been changed since the last time it was backed up. System files are OS/2's own files and they would normally not be altered by a user.

Files that you have marked as Hidden with the File tab can be made to reappear on the desktop by changing the flag test conditions on the Include tab, as described above. However, the Include action affects only the appearance of the desktop. Directory listings made from the OS/2 command prompt will not display hidden files, even when the desktop will.

General Tab

From the General tab you can change the icon used to represent an object on the desktop or in a window. You can either find an icon that already exists on the system, modify the existing one or create one from scratch. To modify the existing icon or create a new one, the Icon Editor is called directly from the Settings notebook. Once you create a new icon and close the Icon Editor, OS/2 immediately replaces the old icon with your new one.

You can utterly confound unauthorized people who might use your system by switching the title and icon of important folders, such as the OS/2 System folder and the Games folder. This can be fun, but it may also be frustrating to legitimate users. Don't do it if there is a chance that a disconcerted user will get angry enough to start throwing things.

CREATING YOUR OWN COLOR SCHEME

We have already discussed how to change the desktop background or the background of a window to the color or bitmapped image of your choice. Backgrounds take up the bulk of the surface area of the screen. However, you can also affect the look of the desktop in more subtle ways that still have an effect on the user's frame of mind.

Believe it or not, there are forty different components to a window. You can assign a custom color to each one of them. Of course some colors do not go well with others. Putting two such colors together can cause eyestrain or mental stress in the user. Even worse would be to assign foreground and background colors that do not have a high degree of contrast. Reading text in such windows can be difficult or impossible.

At any rate, OS/2 gives you the power to exercise your taste, good or bad, to create the appearance that you may be looking at for several hours a day, five or six days a week. To change the default appearance, open the Scheme Palette, which is in the System Setup folder. A window appears (Figure 2-11) showing icons representing ten different color schemes.

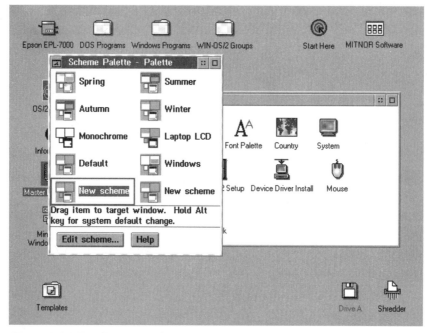

Figure 2-11: The Scheme Palette.

With forty different components scattered all over a window and its associated menus, it is not easy to come up with a combination that is both pleasing to the eye and easy to read. Selecting the wrong color for just one component may render some obscure menu choice unreadable. To help you, OS/2 gives you eight schemes that IBM has tested and found acceptable to large numbers of people. Two additional schemes are provided for you to customize. Actually you may customize all ten if you wish, but it is probably a good idea to leave the preconfigured ones the way they are. One of the eight preprogrammed schemes, named Monochrome, is optimized for monochrome displays that cannot display shades of gray. Another, Laptop LCD, looks good on machines with liquid crystal displays (LCDs). The Windows scheme copies the color scheme of Microsoft Windows. The Default OS/2 color scheme is the one that appears when you first install OS/2.

You can individually assign a color scheme to each window on your desktop, or globally assign one scheme to them all.
It is probably better to maintain a consistent color scheme across all windows.

To select a new color scheme, for example the one labeled "Spring," double-click on its icon on the Scheme Palette. The Edit Scheme dialog box shown in Figure 2-12 will appear.

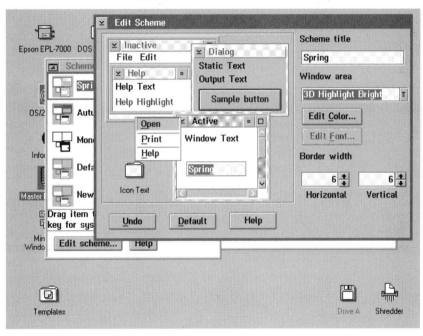

Figure 2-12: The Edit Scheme dialog box.

The box that fills up the left side of the dialog box is the example area. It shows how things look with the selected color scheme. If you want to modify any of the scheme's characteristics, the controls are on the right. You can change the scheme title by typing in a new one. The forty different window components are all listed in the pull-down menu labeled Window area. The current selection is "3D Highlight Bright." To change the 3D Highlight Bright component, select Edit Color. This displays the Edit Color dialog box (Figure 2-13). With it you can mix the contributions of red, green and blue to create one of over 16 million colors. Of course, if your video subsystem is set to display a maximum of 16 colors, much of the power of this feature will not be visible.

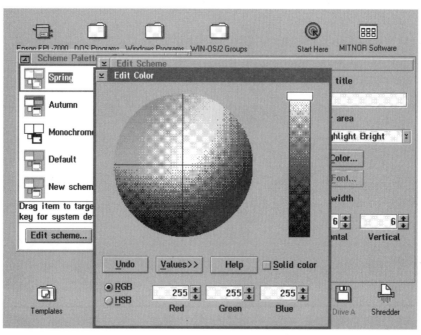

Figure 2-13: Edit Color dialog box.

In addition to changing the colors of window components, you can also change the font of any text that appears in the window. Each different text item is separately controllable, so if you wanted, you could have a mishmash of fonts, some large, some small, some bold, some italic, some serif, some sans-serif. You could make your windows a typographer's nightmare.

Talk about voodoo! You could give users of your system genuine headaches with a judicious choice of clashing fonts and colors from the scheme palette. On the other hand, you could create in them a warm feeling of well-being by making harmonious choices. The decision is yours.

DESKTOP BEHAVIOR—THE SYSTEM SETTINGS

Some of the most fundamental decisions about how an OS/2 system will behave are made by opening the System icon from the System Setup folder. This opens the Settings notebook for the entire system. The notebook has six tabs: Confirmations, Title, Window, Print Screen, Logo and General. The Window and General sections are much the same as the corresponding sections of other windows described earlier. The other sections are unique to the System folder.

Are You Sure?—Soliciting Confirmations

Confirmations are OS/2's best weapons to protect you from your evil twin—that person who deletes files or entire folders that you really want to keep, renames files to something you won't be able to re-member and, in general, creates havoc. This person usually emerges when you have been working too long and are too tired to know exactly what you are doing.

You can decide whether to have OS/2 ask you for confirmation whenever you ask it to perform a potentially damaging action. OS/2's default settings cause it to ask for confirmation whenever you tell it to delete a folder, delete a file or rename a file. It will also display a dialog box showing the progress of an operation that will take more than a second or two. This keeps you from wondering whether the system is hung up or not. By default, OS/2 will not ask for confirmation when you request a copy, move or create shadow operation (more about shadows later in this chapter).

The dialog box that pops up requesting that you confirm your order to make a deletion or perform a rename operation gives your good twin (your true self) a chance to say, "Wait a minute. Do I really want to do this?" If the answer is "NO!," having confirmation activated can save you much grief.

On the other hand, this confirmation business takes extra time and requires your index finger to do extra clicking. If you have your evil twin well under control, you may not want to pay the penalty in time and microjoules of energy that go along with confirmation. In that case you can uncheck the boxes for these selections on the Con-firmations page of the System Settings notebook.

Leave the confirmations in. It is much better to say "NO! I don't want to do this," than it is to say "Noooooooooooo!!!!! I didn't want to do that."

Clash of the Titles—Deciding Who Wins

Sometimes you may, inadvertently or intentionally, try to place an object into a folder that already has an object with the same name. The default action is for OS/2 to inform you of the title clash and ask you what you want to do about it. The title section of the System Settings notebook gives you two other options. One is to automatically rename the new object to something that is very close to the name you tried to give it. The second choice is to replace the existing object in the folder with the new one you are adding. Depending on the type of work you are doing, one of these actions or the other may be appropriate.

 Having OS/2 prompt you for a decision (the default) is always a safe choice.

How Should You Behave When the Window is Open?

The Window tab on the System folder is much like the Window tabs on individual folders, except that the behaviors specified here apply globally rather than to a single folder. Determine whether to show zooming-out-and-in animation when windows are opened and closed, where to send the icons when a window is minimized and whether to redisplay the existing window or create a new one when the icon for an active window is double-clicked.

Print Screen

The Print Screen section has two settings, Enable and Disable. If Enable is selected, pressing your keyboard's Print Screen key when the mouse pointer is not in any specific window will cause the contents of the entire screen to be sent to the printer. If the pointer is in a window, only that window will be sent to the printer.

 Print Screen is a handy utility to have. Generally you will want to leave it enabled, unless you have installed a more sophisticated screen capture utility that you want to supersede it.

Displaying Application Logos

Third-party applications generally identify themselves and their creators by putting a logo and copyright notice on the screen before they start operating. OS/2 gives you the choice of eliminating the logo display completely, displaying it for a specified number of seconds or tenths of seconds and displaying it until the user clicks the OK button or presses a key. If you get tired of waiting for logos to go away, you may want to specify bypassing all logo displays. This possibility sounds great, but some logos will display anyway, no matter what you do with this setting. At least IBM had the right idea.

Tiled Windows or Cascaded?

OS/2 has two completely different ways of displaying windows on the screen: cascaded and tiled. These are in addition to your custom mode of display arrived at by moving and resizing the windows. Your custom layout may involve some overlapping of windows. Figure 2-14 shows a fairly typical layout. Three windows are open. The system clock is small and rather unobtrusive. The other two windows are larger and overlap, but you can still see a good portion of both.

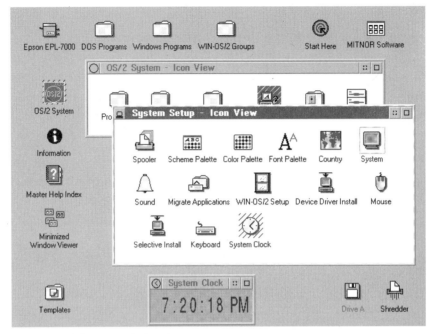

Figure 2-14: Custom window layout.

This works well when only a few windows are open, but when there are a lot, some may be completely obscured. One answer to that problem is to cascade them. To do so, perform this procedure:

1. Press Ctrl+Esc to display the Window List, which lists all currently active windows.

2. With the Ctrl key pressed, click button 1 on all windows you want to cascade.

3. With the pointer located on any of the selected windows in the list, press button 2.

4. From the menu that pops up, press Cascade.

The selected windows will be cascaded (Figure 2-15). The windows overlap each other in a stairstep fashion starting in the upper left corner of the screen. All the windows are the same (large) size, and only the title bars and a strip along the left edge show for all windows except the one on top.

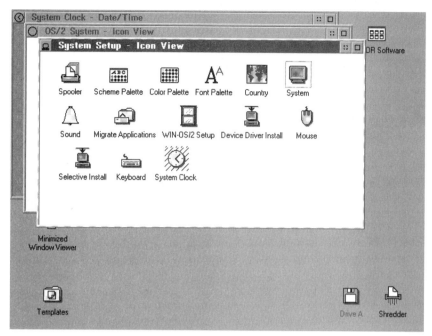

Figure 2-15: Cascaded windows.

Cascaded windows may be for you. This arrangement is good if you want to be sure you know all the windows that are active on the desktop but do not need to see what is in them.

If seeing what is in the windows is important, the tiled arrangement may be what you want. Follow the procedure above for cascaded windows, except at step 4, select Tile rather than Cascade. The result is shown in Figure 2-16. The windows fit together like ceramic tiles on a kitchen counter. Although there is much empty space in the System Setup window and the OS/2 system window, the presence of scroll bars shows that not all objects are displayed.

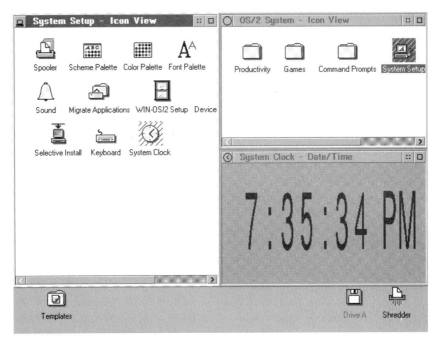

Figure 2-16: Tiled windows.

To rearrange the icons so that as many as possible are displayed, pull down the window's System menu and select Arrange. The icons will be rearranged for best display in the window as it is currently sized and shaped (Figure 2-17).

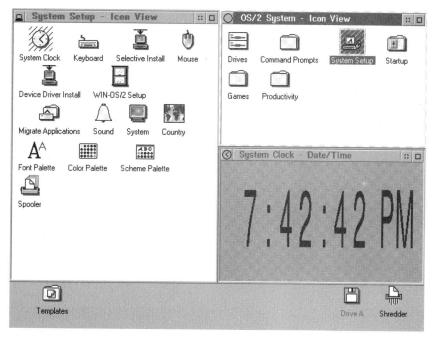

Figure 2-17: Rearranged tiled windows.

SYSTEM CLOCK

Modern personal computers keep track of the current time and date, even when they are unplugged. It takes very little electricity to perform these functions, so a small battery inside the computer maintains the time, date and important configuration information in programmable read-only memory (PROM). OS/2 has access to this time and data information and can display it. Figure 2-14 showed the time displayed at the bottom of the screen in digital format.

The System Clock is one of the resources available from the System Setup folder. Open its Settings notebook to see the options that are available.

Set Your System Clock to Display Date as Well as Time

The first section of the Settings notebook, labeled Date/Time, displays the current time and date. Buttons allow you to change both the time and date maintained in PROM. You can lie to OS/2 about the time and date. Not knowing any better, it will believe you. This feature comes in handy when you are moving your computer to another time zone or even across the international date line.

The second section in the Settings notebook, View, determines the appearance of the clock. You can set it to show time only, date only, or both time and date. You can also decide to show either a digital clock or an analog clock. If you choose the analog display, you may either display or suppress the display of the sweep second hand.

 If you want the clock to be small and unobtrusive on the desktop, but still be readable, the digital display mode is better. After you reduce its size to the minimum that remains easily readable, tuck it in a corner and forget it. You can make it even smaller by unchecking the Show title bar option on the View page. When the title bar disappears, the numerals showing the time will grow larger to fill up the window.

If you suppress the display of the title bar on the system clock (or any other window for that matter), you will not be able to close the window by double-clicking on its system icon at the left end of the title bar. You can still close it by giving it the focus, then pressing Alt+F4. You can also click button 2 anywhere in the window to display its system menu. From there you can open the Settings notebook and check the Show title bar option on the View page to redisplay the title bar.

To display both time and date, select the Both time and date radio button in the Information box on page 1 of the View section. Figure 2-18 shows how the resulting window might look in the upper right corner of the screen.

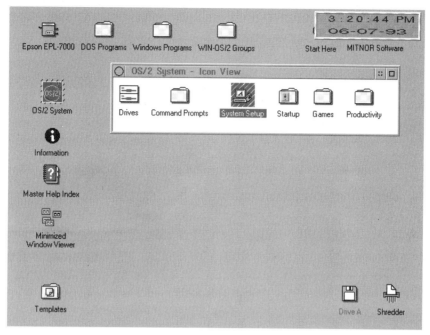

Figure 2-18: System clock displaying both time and date.

Wake Up With the Alarm

The alarm page in the Settings notebook allows you to set an alarm that will go off at the specified time on the specified date. You may choose between an audible alarm that sounds through your computer's speaker or a message box that pops up on the screen. This alarm function is separate and distinct from the Alarms applet available in the Productivity folder.

 Many dangerous and damaging computer viruses are designed to become active and do their damage on a specific date. If you suspect that your computer may be infected with a virus that is due to "go off" on a specific date, make sure that date never comes. On the day before, use the system clock settings notebook to change the date to something different. When midnight rolls around, the computer will think it is a different date. The virus, which after all is a very simple life form, will believe the computer. It will remain quiescent. After the dangerous day is over, you can change your system clock back to the correct date. The virus will continue its slumber, oblivious to the fact that it has been hoodwinked.

COPIES & SHADOWS

It is important to remember that the virtual world we see as the OS/2 desktop is a distorted representation of the hardware and operating software reality that lies underneath. It has been distorted intentionally to make it easier for people to understand and use. Occasionally you may run up against resource limitations that prevent you from doing what you want to do. Often you can get around such limitations by doing things a little differently. It helps if you have some understanding of how the artificial world you see corresponds to the real world that you don't.

On your desktop, program icons and data icons are contained in folders, which themselves may be contained in folders that are higher up in a hierarchy. Each program icon represents an executable file and each data icon represents a data file stored on disk, continually occupying space there. They are loaded into main memory when you call them and take up space there while they are active. Each folder represents a directory on disk that is logically separate from the rest of the disk. An object stored in one directory on disk may have the same name as a different object in a different directory, without OS/2 getting confused. They are maintained as separate entities.

Moving a Desktop Object

You can copy an object from one location on the desktop to another by dragging its icon. There are three kinds of drag, each with a different effect. The first is the simple Move operation. To move an object, click on it with button 1 to select it, then hold button 2 down while you move the mouse to the new folder or desktop location where you want the object to be. When you release the mouse button to complete the drag operation, the object will disappear from its old location and remain in the new one. A Move has no net effect on disk utilization. The program (or folder) you have moved has been copied to its new location and erased from its old one.

Why Copying an Object is Usually a Bad Idea

Copying is similar to moving but with a few small differences. To make a copy, after selecting the object you must hold down the Ctrl key before pressing mouse button 2 to drag it to its new location. Now when you release the mouse button and Ctrl key, the icon for the object remains at its old location as well as being present at the new location. There are now two copies of the object on the desktop and two copies of the underlying file or directory on disk.

A copy of a program in two different folders may lead to consistency problems. If you are using a particular utility program, document or spreadsheet in two entirely different work contexts this may be convenient. Recognize, however, that you are creating a redundancy. If you update one copy but not the other, your data will be out of synchronization. Later it might be difficult to tell which one is right. In any case, making copies will certainly take up extra disk space. There is a better way. In most cases, a shadow will serve just as well as a copy.

Why Creating a Shadow Object is Better

Unlike copies, which are as real as the original and take up disk space, shadows have no independent existence of their own. They are merely aliases for the original object. Like the shadows of Amber, they are but reflections of the one true world. They are, however, always perfect reflections. There is no chance of multiple copies of data getting out of synchronization because there is only one real copy. Even better, shadows take up no disk space.

If you want to use a program or data file in more than one place, create a shadow instead of a copy. To create a shadow, do what you would do to create a copy except hold down both Ctrl and Shift while dragging the object's icon to its new location.

Get rid of unneeded shadow objects by dragging them to the shredder in the lower right corner of the screen and dropping them into it. You drop one icon onto another by releasing button 2 when the appearance of an outline around the destination icon indicates that you are "on target." OS/2 will ask for confirmation of the deletion. When you give it, the dragged object will be deleted. When you drop a "real" object into the shredder, all of its shadows will disappear at the same time. If you shred a shadow, however, its corresponding real object and any other shadows of it will be unaffected.

KEEPING SECRETS

IBM is marketing OS/2 as more than merely a PC operating system. It is designed to control enterprise-wide networks that host mission-critical applications. Corporate management holds such systems to a higher standard than it applies to isolated PCs running simple productivity enhancement applications. For many years mainframe systems have delivered high levels of protection against malicious or inadvertent damage by unauthorized users. As the current trend to downsize computer hardware gathers momentum, the new smaller platforms must provide the same level of security that management has become accustomed to on mainframes. OS/2 has features to address these concerns, features that are completely absent from DOS and any system that runs on top of DOS, such as Windows 3.1.

Locking the Keyboard, Mouse & Display

An excellent way to protect your system from tampering is to deactivate the keyboard, mouse and display. This kind of protection is available from the desktop's Settings notebook. Display the notebook by clicking mouse button 2 anywhere on the desktop that does not contain an icon. When the notebook appears, select the Lockup tab.

The Lockup section has three pages. The first page gives you a choice between no automatic lockup (the default), or automatic lockup after a specified number of minutes have elapsed. You can set the number of minutes to whatever value is best in view of your own personal work habits. Say you have set the Timeout value to five minutes. If you do not depress a keyboard key, click a mouse button or move the mouse for five minutes, the system will automatically lock up.

Page 2 of the section allows you to select a bitmap to display while the system is locked. You may also elect to activate the Auto-dim feature which acts as a screen saver, preventing the CRT's phosphors from burning out prematurely.

On page 3 you enter a password of up to 15 characters. To unlock the system, a person must be able to enter this password. The password is not echoed to the screen when you enter it, so OS/2 asks you to enter it twice to make sure the password you think you have entered is the one you actually have entered.

You can lock up your system immediately if you are about to leave your workstation. Just select Lockup now from the desktop's System menu.

Once your system is locked, it displays the bitmap you selected along with a little padlock icon and a Help button. When you click on the Help button, a dialog box appears instructing you to click on the dialog box's Cancel button, then enter your password.

If you forget your password, you can regain control of the machine by turning it off then on again. It will come up in the unlocked state.

A security system that can be bypassed by simply turning the computer off and on again is pretty weak. This is definitely not mainframe-class protection. There is one thing you can do to strengthen the protection. On page 1 of the Lockup section of the desktop Settings notebook, select Lock on startup. Now if someone tries to bypass your lock by turning the system off and restarting it, they will be disappointed. The system will immediately relock itself as soon as it boots up.

Use a password that you cannot possibly forget. If you use the Lock on startup feature and lose your password, you will be locked out of your system along with everybody else.

OS/2's security system is still rudimentary. It is nowhere near what people have come to expect as standard on mainframe systems. If you require that kind of security, it will have to be built into the applications you are running rather than being a feature of the operating system.

MOVING ON

In this chapter we have covered some of the fundamental customization actions that you can perform to personalize OS/2. With these, you can make your OS/2 environment look very different from that of your neighbor in the next office. There are other customizing actions that you can take as well, which we will encounter in the following chapters when we discuss the various parts of OS/2 in more depth.

Chapter 3
GETTING PROGRAMS TO RUN

O nce OS/2 has been installed and you have customized it to look and behave the way you want, it is time to install the applications that will actually perform useful work. There are now well over a thousand application programs that have been designed specifically to take advantage of OS/2's multithreading capability to run faster and more efficiently than do DOS-based versions of the same programs. In addition to these, nearly all programs written to run under DOS 5.0 (or 6.0) and under Windows 3.1 will run without modification under OS/2.

OS/2-SPECIFIC PROGRAMS

Applications that have been specifically designed to run under OS/2 and take advantage of its power are not as common as those designed to run under DOS and Windows. Nevertheless, there are now several good OS/2 choices in each major application category. For the most popular applications, you may find both a Windows and an OS/2 version. The Windows version will usually run under OS/2.

If you have a choice between acquiring either the Windows or OS/2 version of an application, take the OS/2 version. First, it is guaranteed to run under OS/2. Second, the OS/2 version will often have features lacking in the Windows version, since OS/2 has more capabilities than DOS that developers can use to build more powerful applications. Because of this, the OS/2 version should run faster and more efficiently.

Installing

Installing an OS/2-specific application is a little different from installing a Windows or DOS application. Since the application expects that it is being installed on an OS/2 machine and OS/2 expects that it is installing an OS/2-specific application, the process is simple.

Most applications will be installed from one or more floppy disks, although large applications may come on CD-ROM.

1. There is generally at least one floppy disk that you will place in floppy disk drive A or B. If a CD-ROM is involved, place it in your CD-ROM drive and make sure the drive is working.

2. From the Command Prompts folder, choose OS/2 Window to see a window displaying the OS/2 command prompt ([C:\]).

3. Enter **A:\install** (or **B:\install** if the installation disk is in your B drive, or perhaps **E:\install** if the installation disk is your CD-ROM).

4. Follow the instructions that appear on the screen.

After installation is complete, an icon for your new application's folder should appear on your desktop.

Give your new application folder a distinctive look. When a new folder is added to the desktop it usually has a generic appearance. You can create a more meaningful icon yourself or use one included with the application.

Inside the new application folder will be icons for one or more programs. One of these will probably be the main one and will quickly convey the identity of the application. You can borrow this icon for use on your folder by using the following procedure:

1. Open the new folder to show the icons for the various programs that make up the application.

2. Select the most appropriate icon.

3. Click button 2 on the icon to display its system menu.

4. Choose Open then Settings to display the application's Settings notebook.

5. Click on the General tab to display the current icon.

6. Click on the Edit button to open the Icon Editor, with the new icon displayed in the workspace.

7. Open the Icon Editor's File menu and select Save as...

8. Enter an appropriate name and an .ICO extension, then click on Save. The icon is now in a form that you can use.

9. Return to the desktop and click button 2 on the new folder icon.

10. Select Open and Settings to open the folder's Settings notebook.

11. Click on the General tab to show the current, generic folder icon.

12. Click on Find. OS/2 will search the current directory and display the icons it finds for any files with an .ICO extension.

13. Select the one you just saved with a mouse click, then click on the OK button. The folder's new icon is now displayed.

 Move the icon for your new application folder into a folder that groups it with applications that are logically related.
This will keep your desktop from becoming cluttered with too many icons.

Locating

Locating applications is easy if you have chosen to display the icon for each one on your desktop. Just double-click on the icon and away you go. However, if you have more than a few applications, you probably do not want to fill up the desktop with their icons. It is better to gather groups of related applications into individual folders, which in turn may be placed into a higher level folder.

Do not try to put two objects into the same folder if they have the same names. OS/2 protects you from directly overwriting one with the other by displaying a dialog box. The box asks you whether you want to rename the second object you are putting into the folder or to replace the first object with it. If you rename it, your second application may not work correctly, since it expects the object to have a different name. If you replace the existing object, your first application probably will not work. Either way you lose. Instead, retain the applications in separate folders.

Name your folders in a way that makes sense to you. If you have not used an application for a while and do not remember exactly where it is, you should be able to make a series of very logical folder choices to reach it.

You can still retrieve files, even if you can't find them in the folders on your desktop. In the Productivity folder is an object called "Seek and Scan Files." Double-click on it to display the window shown in Figure 3-1.

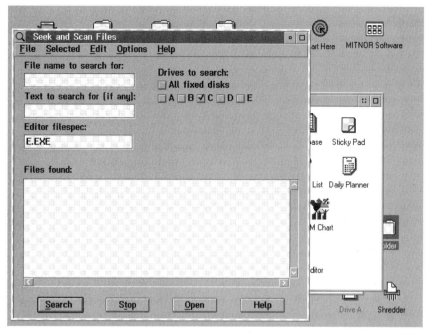

Figure 3-1: The Seek and Scan Files dialog box.

This handy applet will search any or all your disks for the lost file. If you know the name of the file you are looking for, enter it in the field at the top left and click on the Search button. The applet will quickly search the directories of all the drives you specify at the top right, listing all occurrences of the specified file in the Files found: box at the bottom.

If you don't know the name of the file, it will take a little longer to find it. The file you are seeking may contain an uncommon text string. If it does, you can search for that text string in all files on all the disks that are check-marked in the upper right of the dialog box. If several files contain the target string, you should be able to figure out the one you want from the information included in the Files found: window.

If you know what drive your target file is on, specify it under Drives to search:. You can waste a lot of time searching through hundreds of Megabytes of files for the occurrence of a text string. Figure 3-2 shows the result of such a search.

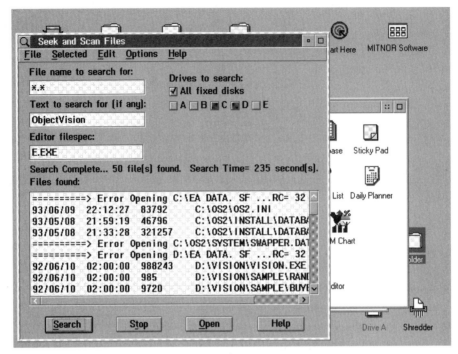

Figure 3-2: Search of all hard drives for text string "ObjectVision."

Two hard drives were searched for the text string "ObjectVision." Fifty files containing the string were found in 235 seconds. The desired file was the source file HELLO.C, which was found on drive D. If you had known that the file was on drive D and searched only that disk, the search would have been completed much sooner. In that case 47 files were found containing "ObjectVision" in 25 seconds (Figure 3-3).

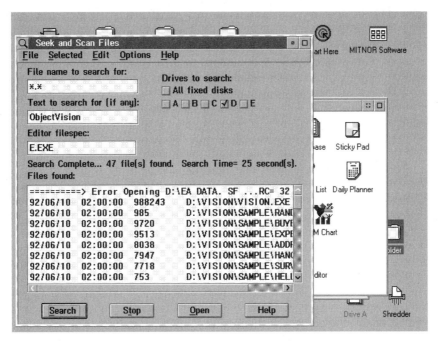

Figure 3-3: A more focused search yields faster results.

This particular search was almost ten times faster when restricted to a single drive. Your mileage may vary depending on the relative sizes of the occupied areas of your drives.

 If the file you are searching for is a text file, you can examine it immediately, without leaving the Seek and Scan Files applet. Notice in Figure 3-3, under Editor filespec:, is E.EXE. This is the file name of OS/2's System Editor. By double-clicking on the HELLO.C line in the Files found: window, you bring up the System Editor in a window, displaying the HELLO.C file. Figure 3-4 shows that window after it has been maximized. Displayed is one possible implementation of the world's most famous computer program. It does indeed contain the word ObjectVision.

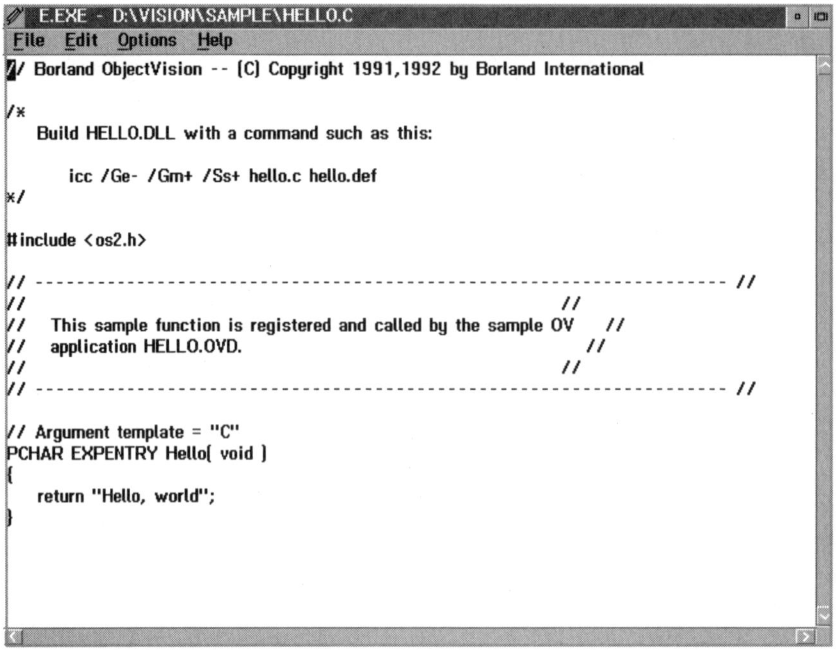

```
/ E.EXE - D:\VISION\SAMPLE\HELLO.C                                    □ ▭
 File  Edit  Options  Help
// Borland ObjectVision -- (C) Copyright 1991,1992 by Borland International

/*
    Build HELLO.DLL with a command such as this:

         icc /Ge- /Gm+ /Ss+ hello.c hello.def
*/

#include <os2.h>

// -------------------------------------------------------------- //
//                                                                //
//    This sample function is registered and called by the sample OV   //
//    application HELLO.OVD.                                       //
//                                                                //
// -------------------------------------------------------------- //

// Argument template = "C"
PCHAR EXPENTRY Hello( void )
{
    return "Hello, world";
}
```

Figure 3-4: The HELLO.C source file as displayed by System Editor from Seek and Scan Files dialog box.

If you know even a little about a file stored somewhere on an OS/2 file system, you will be able to find it. The more you know, the quicker you will succeed.

MIGRATING WINDOWS & DOS PROGRAMS

There are two ways of running Windows applications. One way is by double-clicking WIN-OS/2 Full Screen from the Command Prompts folder. This loads the WIN-OS/2 subsystem, which is a Windows 3.1 emulation that runs under OS/2. It is separate from the rest of OS/2 in the sense that you cannot run a Windows application under WIN-OS/2 at the same time you are monitoring other jobs on the OS/2 desktop. You can, however, quickly switch back to the OS/2 desktop by double-clicking its icon in the lower left corner of the screen.

The second way of running Windows applications is to *migrate* them to OS/2. A migrated Windows application appears in a folder on the OS/2 desktop. You can run it the same way you would run a native OS/2 application. If you run it in a window, you will be able to continue monitoring other events occurring on the desktop.

You can migrate DOS applications the same way you migrate Windows applications. OS/2's migration facility, upon examining an application file, can tell if it is a DOS, Windows or OS/2 application. It will perform whichever migration is appropriate to allow the application to run from the OS/2 desktop.

To install a DOS application on an OS/2 system, select DOS Full Screen from the Command Prompts folder, then follow the installation instructions that come with the application. Once it is installed you should be able to run the application by entering its name at the DOS command prompt.

Although you *should* be able to run full-screen DOS applications by entering their name at the DOS command prompt, sometimes this does not work. Programs that do not run when invoked this way will often run fine if migrated to the Workplace Shell and started by double-clicking on their icon.

To install Windows applications on your OS/2 system, load the WIN-OS/2 Full Screen subsystem. The screen will show a desktop that looks very much like a stock Windows 3.1 desktop. From here, install your application as you would under Windows. Follow the instructions that come with the application. Generally this means to select Run from the File menu, then enter a command line such as "A:\install." This launches the application's installation program. Once installed, the application can be selected and run from the WIN-OS/2 desktop just as you would do it from a "real" Windows 3.1 desktop.

To migrate a Windows application so that you can run it directly from the OS/2 desktop, double-click on Migrate Applications from the System Setup folder, which is contained in the OS/2 System folder. The dialog box shown in Figure 3-5 will pop onto the screen.

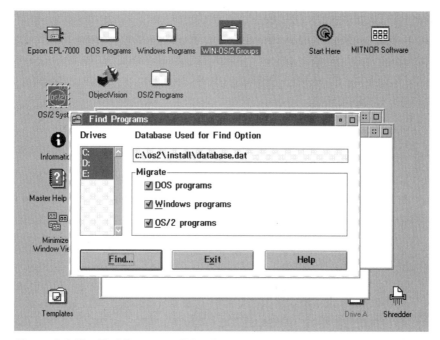

Figure 3-5: The Find Programs dialog box.

All the disks currently installed on the system are shown. DOS, Windows and OS/2 programs are all checkmarked in the Migrate box. If you press the Find... button now, all your disks will be searched for DOS, Windows and OS/2 applications. You can exclude one or more disks from the search by clicking on the disk letter to deselect it. Any applications that are found by the search will be added to a list of migration candidates. The list is displayed in the Migrate Programs dialog box (Figure 3-6).

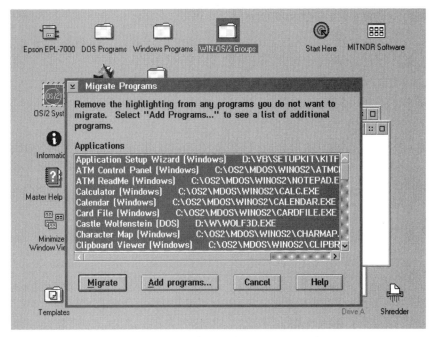

Figure 3-6: Applications found by Migrate Programs search.

You may deselect any of these that you wish. Any that remain when you click on the Migrate button will be migrated to the OS/2 desktop. Icons for DOS applications will be placed in the DOS Programs folder, icons for Windows applications in the Windows Programs folder and icons for OS/2 applications in the OS/2 Programs folder. Applications that were gathered together into Groups under WIN-OS/2 will have their icons placed in the WIN-OS/2 Groups folder.

LAUNCHING

Once an application has been installed, it will sit on your desktop doing nothing until you actually try to run it.

There are numerous ways to start an application. You may try using your favorite magical incantation. If you combine it with one of the techniques listed below, onlookers may actually believe that you do have the power of voodoo.

Double-clicking on a Desktop Icon

If the application you want to launch is one you use frequently, you may find it convenient to have its icon directly on the desktop. All you need to do is double-click the mouse pointer on it to start the application.

If you move the mouse ever so slightly between the first and second click of your double-click, OS/2 will not interpret it as a double-click. It will select the icon, but nothing more. If this happens, try again, taking care to hold the mouse very still.

Launching From a Group Folder

Often application suites have several executable components. These would typically be grouped together into a folder bearing the name and icon of the overall application. When you double-click on the folder's icon, it displays a window showing icons for all the components. Pick the one you want and double-click on it.

Launching From a Program Folder

Earlier when we talked about migrating applications to OS/2, we mentioned that the migrated "apps" are placed in folders on the desktop. DOS programs are placed in a folder named DOS Programs. Windows programs are placed in a folder named Windows Programs. Groups of related programs that started life together in a Windows folder are migrated to a folder named WIN-OS/2 Groups. And finally, you guessed it, OS/2 programs are placed in a folder named OS/2 Programs. Thus OS/2 programs that are accessible either directly on the desktop or in a group folder on the desktop are also present in the OS/2 Programs folder and can be launched from there. Figure 3-7 shows two ways of launching the ObjectVision application.

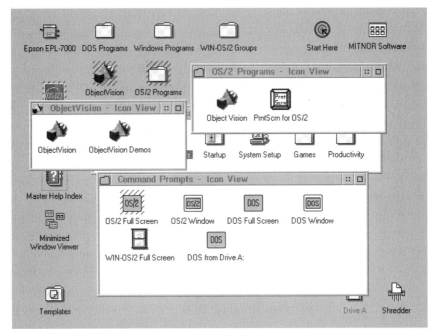

Figure 3-7: Launching an application using its icon.

The ObjectVision icon on the desktop represents a folder containing two executable programs, ObjectVision and ObjectVision Demos, both shown in the window below the desktop ObjectVision icon. The OS/2 Programs folder holds two applications, ObjectVision and PrntScrn for OS/2. The window for this folder is to the right of its icon. By double-clicking on the ObjectVision icon in either of the displayed windows, the program will start.

You can launch multiple instances of an application by double-clicking on its desktop icon more than once (Figure 3-8). This works only if the Create new window option on the Window page of the object's Settings notebook is selected.

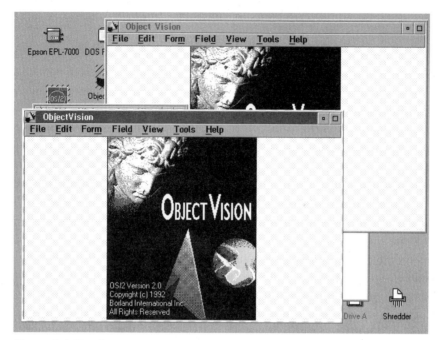

Figure 3-8: Two instances of an application running simultaneously.

If you do launch multiple instances of an application and are dealing with the same data files, you may cause an unwanted interaction between the two sessions. If you are going to run multiple applications (and if you are not, you might as well stick with DOS), it is best to make sure they are not operating on the same files at the same time.

Starting DOS Applications Full Screen as Opposed to in a Window

In the Command Prompts folder there are three possible DOS environments, DOS Full Screen, DOS Window and DOS from Drive A:. Since DOS does not have a graphical user interface that makes use of windows, many applications written for DOS take over the entire screen. Such applications will not run in a DOS window. Other DOS applications will run without problems in a window.

If you are running a DOS application under OS/2 for the first time, run it full-screen. Confirm that it runs without problems in that screen mode. Then, if you would like to be able to run it in a window, try starting it from the DOS prompt in a windowed session. If it works, great! If not, you can fall back to running it full-screen. Use DOS from Drive A: to run those few applications that will not even run properly with OS/2's full-screen DOS emulation. You can put a copy of "real" DOS on a floppy disk and insert it into drive A. Your DOS from Drive A: session will boot and you can run your environmentally sensitive DOS application.

Using Key Combinations to Select & Launch

Although it's a lot more cumbersome, you can start any application without using a mouse. Anything that can be done with the mouse can also be done using only the keyboard.

The application you want to start is either on the desktop or inside a folder that is on the desktop. Follow this procedure:

1. Press Alt+Shift+Tab to select the desktop. One of the icons on the desktop will be highlighted, indicating that it is currently selected. Probably the selected object (the last one you accessed) is not the one you want.

2. Hold the Shift key down while you press the cursor movement arrow keys. Pressing the Left arrow key will select the icon to the left of the current one. Pressing the Up arrow key will select the icon above the current one, and so on. By pressing the proper arrow keys in succession, you will be able to select the icon for your application or the folder that holds it.

3. Press the Enter key to open the selected object. If the object you just opened is your application, you are home free. The application is now running.

4. If the object you just opened is a folder, use Shift and the arrow keys to select the object within the folder that you want, then press Enter to open it.

5. Repeat step 4 as needed to open all the layers of nested folders until you finally reach the application itself and open it.

Don't spend a lot of time memorizing these keystroke combinations. Use the keyboard to navigate around the desktop and start applications only if your mouse suddenly stops working and you need to get some work done before you have a chance to buy a new one. Otherwise, use the mouse.

The OS/2 Full-Screen Command Prompt

When you open the OS/2 Full Screen icon from the Command Prompts window, you are taken back to those glorious days of yesteryear when users were confronted with a blank screen, punctuated only by a drive-identifying prompt. Those were the days when getting anything useful out of a computer really did seem like voodoo to the uninitiated. You had to enter arcane commands with obscure syntax in order to get applications to run.

The architects of OS/2 have thoughtfully provided us with that same command prompt interface that caused many people a decade ago to conclude that they would never "learn computers." Actually the command prompt interface can be useful. It provides a more direct path to the system hardware than does the Workplace Shell. Once you learn the most commonly used commands, it's often easier to perform operations from the command prompt than it is from the desktop. Happily it's easy and fast to switch between the two.

A number of common operations can be performed more quickly from the command prompt than from the desktop. It's worth the effort to learn the syntax of the various forms of the directory, format, copy and rename commands. Often it will be easier to use them than the Workplace Shell equivalents.

The OS/2 Window Command Prompt

The environment provided by the OS/2 Window command prompt is the same as that of its full-screen brother except that it appears in a resizable window rather than taking up the whole screen. The desktop can clearly be seen behind the window.

If you are cramped for space in a command prompt window, you can always maximize the window. In VGA mode this makes it effectively identical to the OS/2 full-screen command prompt.

Automatically Launching Applications With the Startup Folder

Under DOS if you want to start a particular application every time you boot the operating system, put its name into the AUTOEXEC.BAT file. All statements in that file are executed every time DOS is started, before control is turned over to the user. OS/2 gives you the same capability, and more, with its Startup folder.

The Startup folder is located in the OS/2 System folder. At first it is empty but you can move, copy or shadow objects into it. Every application in it is opened at startup time, before control is given to the user.

Place whatever applications you wish into the Startup folder by dragging them from their normal location. To be more efficient, drag the application's shadow into the Startup folder. Every application represented in the Startup folder will be opened at boot time.

The Startup folder is better than the old AUTOEXEC.BAT in that it also retains your current operating environment and restores it the next time you boot up.

The Workplace Shell remembers what applications were open the last time you shut down and automatically opens them again the next time you boot. Part of OS/2's shutdown procedure is to place shadows of all open applications into the Startup folder. With this feature, you can pick up immediately where you left off without having to reopen your applications.

To add an object to your Startup folder, follow these directions:

1. Open the Startup folder in the OS/2 System folder. Unless someone has already added something to it, it will be empty.

2. Place the mouse cursor on the icon for the object you want to open at boot time.

3. Press Ctrl+Shift and mouse button 2, then drag the icon into the Startup folder. A duplicate icon will appear, connected to the original by a line.

4. Release mouse button 2, then release Ctrl and Shift. The duplicate icon will now be in the Startup folder and will be selected.

5. Close the Startup window by double-clicking on its close widget (the System menu icon). The next time you boot OS/2, the application you have shadowed in the Startup folder will be automatically opened and ready for your immediate use.

You can remove an object from the Startup folder the same way you remove any object from the desktop, by dragging it to the Shredder and dropping it in.

1. Place the mouse cursor on top of the object you want to delete and press mouse button 2.

2. Drag the object to the Shredder, which is usually located in the lower right corner of the desktop.

3. When the dragged object is centered over the Shredder, release the mouse button. As a safety precaution the Delete Object(s) dialog box will appear (Figure 3-9).

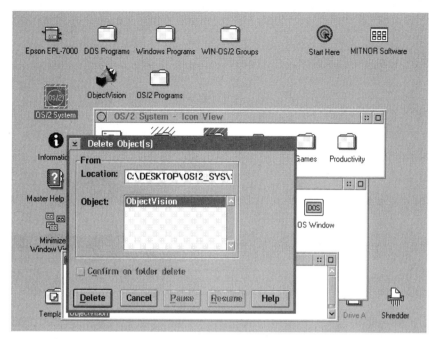

Figure 3-9: The Delete Object(s) dialog box.

Since deleting an object is potentially an irrevocable act, OS/2 gives you the opportunity to reconsider your decision. You must click on the Delete button to proceed. You can abort the deletion by clicking on Cancel instead. In our example the deletion is not irrevocable, since we are only deleting a shadow. No actual files will be deleted.

4. Click on Delete to remove the shadow object from the Startup folder. The next time you boot up, the removed object will not be automatically started.

Closing Applications

Clearly, opening applications is very important, since you cannot do any useful work without opening an application. However, closing applications is important too. Open applications consume system memory. If too many are open, you will not be able to continue working. When you close an application it returns the memory it had been using to the operating system.

Some applications may not return all their allocated memory to OS/2 when they close. This problem is called "memory leakage." If you run a program that suffers from a memory leak, you will find yourself running out of memory if you repeatedly open and close the program during a session. Deduce which application is causing the problem and call its vendor to see if there is a fix for it.

Well-behaved applications behave the way you expect them to. They are easy to close. Any application running in an OS/2 window can be closed by double-clicking its close widget in the upper left corner of its window. In addition, many applications have a pull-down menu that has an Exit choice. Selecting it will terminate processing of the application as well.

WIN-OS2 applications may also be closed either from their close widget or from a menu choice. Full-screen DOS applications have a variety of ways of closing down; you should consult the documentation of each program. Regardless of which of these methods is used, the well-behaved application will be closed and all its memory returned to the system for redeployment to other applications.

Sometimes things go wrong, and you lose control of an application. For example, if you try to start a mandatory full-screen application in a window, the result may be a blank screen and an application that is "hung." Under DOS or Windows 3.1 you would be out of luck. You would have to press the Reset button and lose everything you had in memory. OS/2, because of its logical isolation of applications in separate memory spaces, gives you a chance to recover from such a problem.

If you press both mouse buttons at the same time, or Ctrl+Esc on the keyboard, the window list will pop up. It lists all the processes that are currently active. The application that is locked up will be on the list. Put the mouse pointer on the offending application and press button 2. A menu will pop up that includes the Close option. Click on Close. The renegade application will close and you can proceed.

The problems caused by a renegade application can escape the application's assigned memory space and affect other applications or even OS/2 itself. In those cases, the system freezes in the same way that a DOS/Windows 3.1 system would. Resetting then would be the only way out.

To close an application without a mouse, press Alt+F4.

SHUTTING DOWN OS/2

Don't just turn your machine off when you are finished working. OS/2 is doing a lot of things "under the surface" in addition to the more obvious task of allowing your application to run. When you finish your work and close the application you have been working on, other operations may not be complete. There may be information in memory that needs to be written to disk. To handle this situation, the desktop's pop-up menu has a Shut down option.

Use the desktop's pop-up menu to do an ordinary shutdown. Click mouse button 2 anywhere on the desktop where there is not an object. From the pop-up menu that appears, click on Shut down. OS/2 will do the necessary housekeeping, then display a message telling you it is OK to turn off or reboot your computer.

Shutting down OS/2 while windows are still open makes it easy for you to pick up where you left off. OS/2 preserves the status of the desktop and reopens it to the same condition the next time you turn on your machine.

You can still shut down OS/2 when you don't have a mouse. People operating without a mouse cannot click button 2 on the desktop, since they have no button 2. They can still do an orderly shutdown by following this procedure:

1. Press Ctrl+Esc to display the Window List.

2. Use arrow keys to move the cursor to "Desktop - Icon View."

3. Press Enter to select the desktop.

4. Press Ctrl+\ to deselect all.

5. Press Shift+F10 to display the desktop's pop-up menu.

6. Select Shut down.

 If you shut down while an ill-behaved (renegade) process is active, it will cause a failure every time you try to boot up. We noted earlier in this chapter that you can usually close a renegade process by popping up the window list and closing it from there. If you forget to do that, the next time you boot, OS/2 will restart all the applications that were active when you shut down, including the ill-behaved one. It will still be out of control.

 If an ill-behaved application was active the last time you shut down, press Ctrl+Shift+F1 as soon as the clock face appears the next time you boot up. Keep all three keys depressed until the desktop stabilizes. This key combination prevents all of the applications that were active on the last shutdown from loading. You can now selectively open applications, carefully avoiding the offending one until you have fixed the problem with it.

 If you are not sure how to cure the renegade application but have several solutions in mind, try them one by one, rebooting in between with Ctrl+Shift+F1 pressed. Hopefully one idea will work and you will be able to use the rehabilitated application again.

MEMORY MANAGEMENT

One of OS/2's valuable features is its automatic memory management. If you are running multiple applications, each with its own memory requirements, you do not need to keep track of how much memory is already in use before launching another application. In fact, OS/2 can allocate more memory than is physically installed in your system.

OS/2 memory management makes use of *virtual memory*. Virtual memory is not really there, but acts as if it is. It seems like there must be voodoo at work here, but actually there is a logical explanation.

There are two kinds of computer memory. First there is *system memory*. This is made up of read only memory (ROM), and read/write memory (also called RAM for random access memory). This is what people usually refer to when they talk about a computer's memory. A 16mb computer has that amount of system memory. System memory is very fast and is instantly available.

Computers also have a slower form of memory called *on-line storage*. This is the memory on hard disks or CD-ROM drives. Tens or hundreds of megabytes are typical sizes for on-line memory. People don't usually use the term memory for on-line storage, but it is memory, nonetheless.

A virtual memory system sets aside some of the storage on hard disk, which then becomes unavailable for user files. This area is called the swap file and is used as an extension of the system memory. When the system memory is full of active sessions and you start another one, OS/2's memory management logic swaps out to disk the least recently used segment of system memory to make room for the new task. If one of your applications then requires the swapped code, it is swapped back in and something else is sent to disk. In this way, the most active code and data segments are kept in system memory and the least active on disk. Since system memory is much faster than disk memory, this strategy gives the best overall performance.

Make sure your computer has enough system memory so that swapping is a rare occurrence. Swapping is a tremendous advantage on those occasions when you want to do something that is just a little beyond the capability of your hardware. However, if you rely on it too heavily, your performance will be drastically reduced.

Memory chips are cheap. If you are swapping a lot, buy more of them to reduce swapping and improve performance.

OS/2 maintains a file on disk named SWAPPER.DAT. It contains any overflow from system memory. You can set a starting size for the swap file, but it will grow beyond that if your applications keep demanding more storage. In fact, the swap file will grab all the free space on your hard disk if you let it, leaving none for new files.

When you first install OS/2, a configuration file (CONFIG.SYS) is built for you. It will contain a statement similar to the following:

```
SWAPPATH=C:\OS2\SYSTEM 2048 1024
```

This means that SWAPPER.DAT will be located in the directory OS2\SYSTEM on hard disk drive C. It will have a starting size of 1024 kilobytes and may grow larger. The first parameter requires that it leave at least 2048 kilobytes free.

Pay attention to swap file warning messages. If the swap file grows to the point where there is less than the specified amount of free disk space left (2048 KB in this case), a warning will tell you to close some jobs or create more free space on the disk by erasing unneeded files. If you ignore this warning and the swap file continues to grow, it may collide with your disk files with disastrous results. You will probably lose data.

MOVING ON

In this chapter we have seen that you can install a variety of types of applications under OS/2 and run them in a variety of ways. Applications migrated from DOS and Windows are important in OS/2, but they will become progressively less so as more OS/2-specific applications reach the market.

Much of the discussion in this chapter made reference to the Workplace Shell. In the next chapter we will take a detailed look at the WPS and some of the magic that can be performed with it.

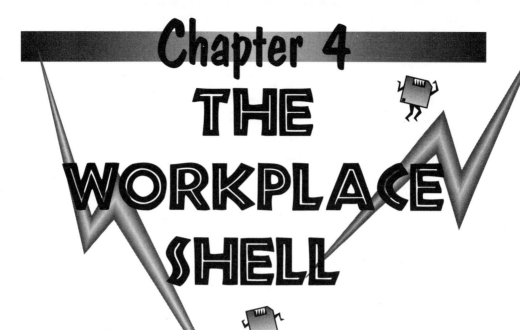

Chapter 4
THE WORKPLACE SHELL

The Workplace Shell is the visible part of OS/2. It is the outside layer of the operating system that shields the user from the complexities underneath. The Workplace Shell (WPS) makes the facilities of OS/2 available to people who have not mastered the OS/2 command language. Even those who *have* mastered the language are able to perform most operations more quickly and easily using the WPS than by issuing commands directly.

SETTING UP THE LOOK & FEEL

The default appearance of the Workplace Shell on the desktop was selected, after much research, because it is a comfortable, easy-to-use environment for a broad cross-section of people. This does not, however, mean that it is the best work environment for you. IBM built the WPS so you can customize many of its visible aspects. The principal tool for this customization is the Settings notebook.

Settings Notebooks for Folders

In previous chapters we have seen the Settings notebook used to adjust mouse and keyboard settings. Every OS/2 object has a related

Settings notebook that controls many aspects of the way the object is displayed. The content of Settings notebooks varies, depending on what kind of objects they control. Folders have different settings requirements than applications.

OBJECT ARRANGEMENT IN A FOLDER

One thing you may want to change about a folder is the way its objects are displayed. The default arrangement, shown in Figure 4-1, is called the Non-grid arrangement. Icons are arranged in rows with their names underneath. The spacing between icons depends on the width of the icon names.

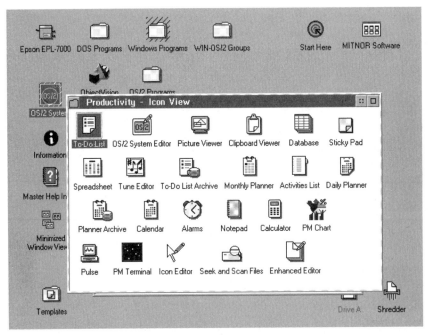

Figure 4-1: The Productivity folder with Non-grid arrangement.

By opening the Settings notebook and changing the default Non-grid arrangement to Flowed (Figure 4-2), a very different display results (Figure 4-3).

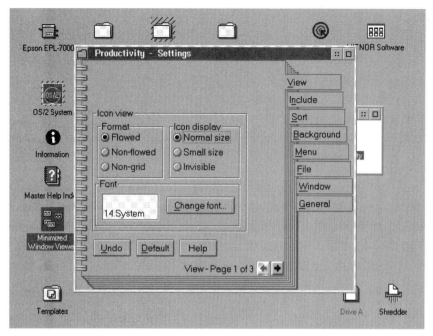

Figure 4-2: The View page of the Productivity folder Settings notebook.

Figure 4-3: The Productivity folder with Flowed arrangement.

The object names are now in a larger font and located to the right of their icons. This arrangement takes up more space than the Non-grid format, so the window must be larger to display all the objects.

The third choice, Non-flowed, displays all the icons in a single vertical column. You can make the window narrower without obscuring any icons. Since the icons are all in a single column, there is not enough room on the screen to display them all. A vertical scroll bar has been added to give access to those off the top of the screen (Figure 4-4).

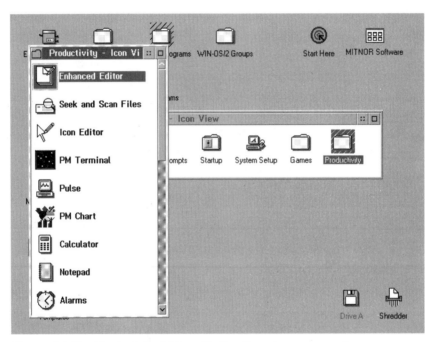

Figure 4-4: The Productivity folder with Non-flowed arrangement.

Set your folders up to have the arrangement you prefer. IBM's default choice of Non-grid is appropriate for people who like to view things in horizontal rows. Non-flowed is better for people who prefer vertical columns of information. Flowed is the most readable for people who are more text-oriented than icon-oriented.

You can change the icon view format of your existing folders by opening their Settings notebook and changing the settings.

 You can change the default from Non-grid to your choice of Flowed or Non-flowed in all future folders that you create. Do this by changing the icon view format setting in the Settings notebook of your Folder template. Templates are discussed later in this chapter. After making the change to the template, any folders you create with it will automatically display icons in the format you have chosen.

If you're using the default Non-grid arrangement, don't select Arrange from the desktop's pop-up menu. If you do, the WPS will obliterate your carefully considered placement of objects and place them all in rows at the top of the screen (Figure 4-5). Some people may prefer this arrangement, but if you want to order your icons in functional groups, don't select Arrange.

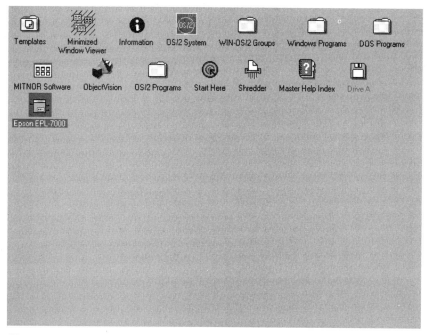

Figure 4-5: The desktop after Arrange is selected.

SETTING A NEW BACKGROUND

The backgrounds of windows are normally set to a light solid color so that any icons and text displayed will have high contrast and be easy to see. However, you can fill the background with dark colors and distracting patterns. For example, the desktop itself is a window and its background can be set from its Settings notebook in the same way as other windows. Figure 4-6 shows the desktop after its background has been changed to the BUTTERFLY.BMP bitmap provided with OS/2. The effect is rather soothing, but the icons on the desktop are nearly impossible to see.

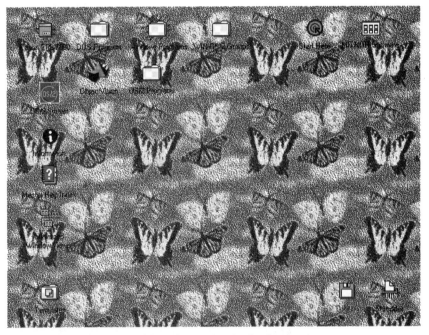

Figure 4-6: The desktop with an image for the background.

Stick with solid colors for window backgrounds. The reduced eyestrain will result in fewer headaches and big savings on ophthalmologist bills.

ADDING APPLICATIONS TO A MENU

Selecting and activating a program's icon with either the mouse or the keyboard are not the only ways to launch an application. You can also add the application as an option to any object's pop-up menu. Since the desktop is a folder that is always open, you may want to add frequently used applications to its menu.

As an example, let's say you want to add the Reversi game to the desktop's pop-up menu so that at any moment you get the urge to play a quick game, you can satisfy the craving with a few mouse clicks. Follow this procedure:

1. Click mouse button 2 on an empty spot on the desktop to display its pop-up menu.

2. Select Open from the menu, then Settings from the submenu.

3. At the desktop's Settings notebook, click on the Menu tab. The notebook page shown in Figure 4-7 will appear.

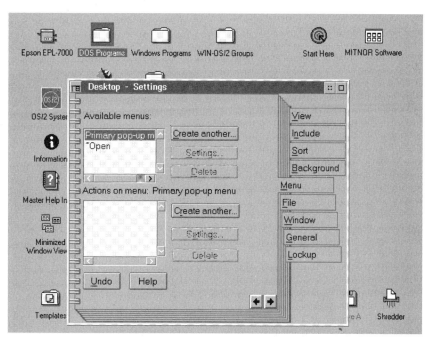

Figure 4-7: The desktop's Menu Settings page.

4. Make sure that under Available menus: Primary pop-up menu is selected.

5. Under Actions on menu: Primary pop-up menu, click on the Create another... button. The Menu Items Settings dialog box will pop onto the screen.

6. Fill in "Reversi" in the Menu item name: field. If you know the exact name of the executable file, enter it into the Name: field in the Program box. If you don't, click on the Find program... button.

7. If you use Find, you will be asked to specify what you know about the target file. OS/2 will display icons for all objects that meet your criteria. You should be able to select the appropriate one from the list.

8. After you select the icon for the program you want, the result will be shown in the Menu Items Settings dialog box (Figure 4-8). You are asked to confirm the new setting.

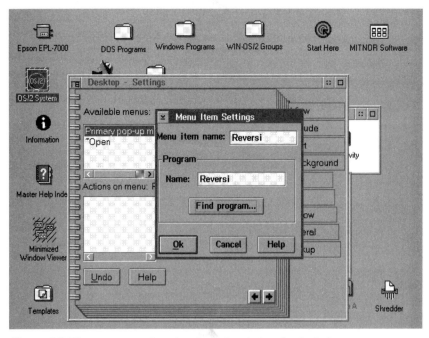

Figure 4-8: The new menu item has been located and selected.

9. Click OK to accept the new setting. You are returned to the Settings notebook Menu page shown in Figure 4-9. The new menu option is already in effect.

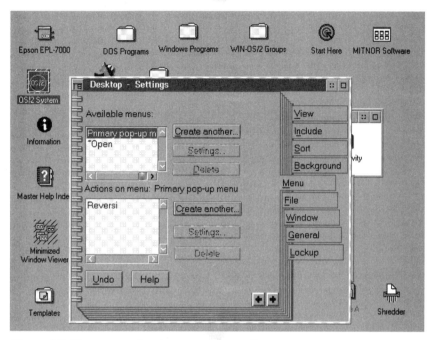

Figure 4-9: Menu page showing new menu option.

10. Double-click on the Settings notebook's close widget to banish the notebook from the desktop.

11. Click button 2 on a blank spot on the desktop. The desktop's menu appears, with the new Reversi option at the bottom (Figure 4-10).

12. When you click on the new option, the Reversi game opens and takes up a central position on the screen.

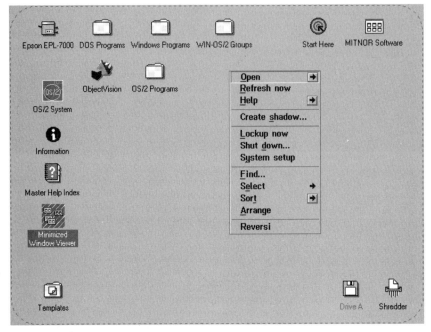

Figure 4-10: Modified desktop menu.

 There is another, even faster way to add an application to a menu. For this method to work:

1. Find the icon for the application you want to add to a menu and display it on the desktop.

2. Follow steps 1 through 4 from the procedure above.

3. Drag your application's icon into the list box under Actions on menu: Primary pop-up menu (Figure 4-11). The dragged icon will be grayed out. When you release button 2, the name of the application will have been added to the list box.

4. Close the notebook. The new menu choice is already present on the target menu.

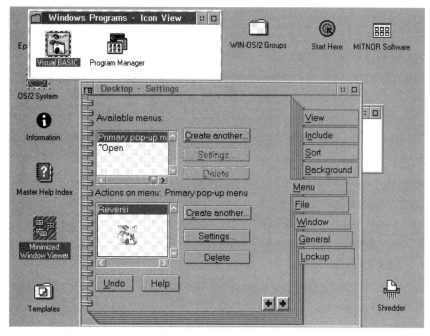

Figure 4-11: Create a menu choice by icon dragging.

Icons

Icons are critically important to the use of the Workplace Shell. A good icon will immediately bring to mind the object that it represents. It should also be different enough from other icons on the desktop to minimize confusion.

Commercial applications often have colorful, professionally designed and painstakingly rendered icons. On the other hand, the default icons OS/2 provides for programs that do not have their own are dull, gray, uninspiring and the same as all the other default icons. You will probably want to replace any such icons on your system.

Of course you can use the Icon Editor to create new icons, but many of us are not skilled artists, and our efforts may turn out to be less than satisfactory. We can follow the example of Sir Isaac Newton (1643-1727), considered by many to have the greatest scientific mind of all time. Newton's genius was recognized in his lifetime and he received many honors. On one occasion, he sought to pass around some of the credit for his accomplishments. "If I have seen farther than others," he said, "it is because I have stood on the shoulders of giants." The giants he was referring to were Copernicus, Galileo and Kepler among others. Newton's most important insights were based on information that had been provided by these other scientists. You can do the same thing. There is no need to draw your own icons when thousands exist in the public domain.

Become a member of CompuServe and join the OS2USER forum. In the forum's libraries are several thousand icons appropriate to just about any conceivable situation. Download the ones you want and use them.

Download Dave Lester's Shareware utility IconEase from OS2USER library 4. It will make it easy for you to pull the needle of the exact icon you need from the haystack of the thousands that are available.

MANIPULATING OBJECTS

Once you are satisfied with the look and feel of your system, it is a good idea to master the use of desktop objects before adding production applications to the system. There are many things you can do with a Workplace Shell object, but before you can do anything else, you must select it.

Selecting Objects

Selecting a visible object on the desktop is easy if you have a mouse. Just place the pointer on top of the object and press button 1. The border of the object will reverse color, showing it has been selected.

Without a mouse, selecting is a little more involved. To place the pointer on the object, first you must get into the proper window. Once in the window, you must move to the desired object. Follow this procedure:

1. Press Ctrl+Esc to show the Window List.

2. If the object you want to select is listed, use the arrow keys to put the cursor on it, then press Enter to select it.

3. If the object you want is not listed but the folder that contains it is, select the folder by putting the cursor on it and pressing Enter. Then press the arrow keys to select the object. Press Enter to open the selected object.

4. If the object you want is not listed and the folder that contains it is also not listed, select the desktop from the Window List. Use the arrow keys to move the selection from its current location on the desktop to the folder that contains your object. Press Enter to open the folder. Now use the arrow keys to select the desired object.

Selecting Multiple Objects

There are several ways to select multiple objects in a window. Press Ctrl and click mouse button 1 on the objects you want to select. As each icon is added to the selection, the background surrounding it reverses in color.

If you don't have a mouse, you can select multiple objects in a window with the keyboard alone. First press Shift+F8 to put the window into multiple select mode. Next, use the arrow keys to move the selection rectangle to the icon you want to select. Press the space bar to select it. When you have selected all the objects you want, you may press Enter to open them, or you may perform other operations. Press Shift+F8 again to leave multiple select mode.

Formatting Floppy Disks—The Drive A Object

One of the primary reasons for selecting multiple objects is to move or copy them to another disk as a group. Backing up recently changed files to a floppy disk is a common reason to perform a multiple object copy operation. Often you will want to format a floppy disk before copying files to it. The Drive A object's pop-up menu has an option for formatting diskettes.

Format diskettes using the Drive A icon.

1. To format a diskette, place it into drive A, then click button 2 on the Drive A icon to display its pop-up menu.

2. Select Format disk. The Format Disk A: dialog box appears.

3. Enter a volume label if desired and select the proper capacity. OS/2 is smart enough to know whether drive A is a 3.5-inch or a 5.25-inch drive and only allows you to choose from the options that are appropriate for the size you have.

4. Click on the Format button. A dialog box showing progress will be displayed until the operation is complete. At that point it will display the number of bytes available.

Moving Objects

To move an object, put the mouse pointer on it, press button 2 and drag it to its new location. Release button 2 when you arrive. The object is now absent from its old location and present at its new one.

You can move an object you no longer want to the Shredder. When you drop it in, it will be destroyed. If you drop an original object (as opposed to a copy or shadow) into the Shredder, the WPS will ask for confirmation before erasing it.

To move a window, put the mouse pointer on its title bar and press button 2. Now drag the window anywhere you want.

It is possible for a window whose title bar is completely out of sight to still appear on the screen. This situation (Figure 4-12) can happen if you have changed to a high resolution display such as 1024x768, then changed back to a lower resolution display such as 640x480. If you resized or relocated a window at the higher resolution, it may show up partially off-screen at the lower resolution. Since you cannot see the title bar, you cannot put a pointer on it to move the window to make it fully visible. This would be a serious problem if there weren't a keyboard equivalent for every mouse action under OS/2.

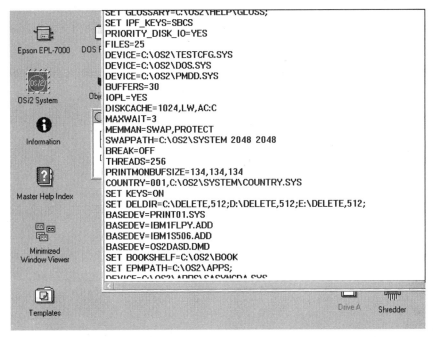

Figure 4-12: Top of a window is off the screen.

If you want to move a window but cannot see its title bar, select it, then press Alt+F7. Now when you use the arrow keys, a phantom outline of the window will move correspondingly. Move it enough to display the title bar and to resize it for the current screen resolution. Press Enter to return from move mode to normal desktop operation.

Copying Objects

After you copy an object, you end up with two objects, one at the original location and one at the new location. The action is similar to moving an object. To copy an object, hold down the Ctrl key while you drag the icon from the source to the destination.

You can't copy an object to the Shredder. What would be the point? The original would still exist.

 You can copy an object to the desktop or to most folders on the desktop.

You cannot copy to the Minimized Window Viewer or the Master Help Index. In fact, when you try to copy to a forbidden destination, the WPS will display a horizontal bar symbol similar to the "DO NOT ENTER" traffic sign to show that copying is not allowed.

You can't copy some objects to Drive A by dropping them on the Drive A icon. In these cases, you will be faced with the "DO NOT ENTER" symbol.

Creating Objects

The WPS desktop plays host to a rich array of objects, including programs, folders, data files, printers and palettes. Commercial applications normally include program and data files and sometimes bitmaps, pointers and PIF files. Such applications have automatic installation procedures that put all the application's files into a folder it creates.

Rather than clutter up your desk with lots of folders, you may want to put several of your most frequently used applications into a single folder. To do this, you will need to create a new folder. You do not need to specify every detail of your new folder. OS/2 provides a set of templates that specify default characteristics for a dozen different types of objects. Open the Templates folder to see them.

CREATING OBJECTS USING TEMPLATES

When you open the Templates folder, you will see templates for all the major types of WPS objects (Figure 4-13). In addition to these templates, some applications provide their own, which they add to the Templates folder when they are installed.

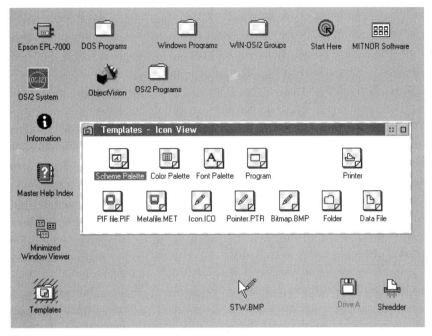

Figure 4-13: Templates for standard WPS objects.

To create a new folder using one of the templates in the Template folder, perform the following procedure:

1. Display the Template folder window shown in Figure 4-13.

2. Find the Folder template in the Template folder window (confusing, isn't it?) and copy it to the desktop using Ctrl+drag.

3. Click button 2 on the newly copied icon to display its pop-up menu.

4. Select Open, then Settings to show its Settings notebook.

5. Go through all the tabs, setting things to your preferences.

6. On the General tab, uncheck the Template check box. This tells the WPS that this instance of the folder template is a standard folder, not a template. Also give the folder a new title that is specific to the new purpose to which you will put it.

You can now open the folder and put either objects or shadow objects into it.

Templates use disk space, memory space and increase OS/2's load time. If new applications put templates into your Templates folder, you may notice load time increasing and disk space diminishing. Delete templates that you are absolutely certain you will never use.

CREATING OBJECTS WITHOUT USING TEMPLATES

Many times you do not need the templates in the Template folder. You can use any already existing object to serve as a template for a similar object that you want to create.

Use an existing object as a template rather than one of the standard templates in the Templates folder. If you already have an object that is closer to the one you want than any of the generic templates in the Templates folder, use it. Open its Settings notebook, and under the General tab, check the Template box. *Voilà!* It is now a template. You can peel off an unlimited number of copies of it simply by performing move operations. After you have finished, you can uncheck the Template box to return it to its former status as an ordinary object.

Creating Shadow Objects

We have already referred to shadow objects several times. They look like extra copies of an original object, but they are not. Rather than having an independent existence of their own like a copy, they are pointers to the original object.

It can be handy to have shadows of frequently used objects in a folder where you do much of your work. The locations of the original objects does not matter. When you manipulate the shadow object, you automatically manipulate the original at the same time.

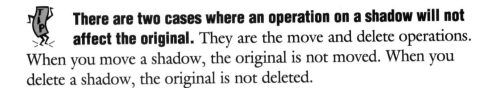

There are two cases where an operation on a shadow will not affect the original. They are the move and delete operations. When you move a shadow, the original is not moved. When you delete a shadow, the original is not deleted.

Deleting Objects

Deleting most objects is fairly straightforward. Two common ways of doing it from the WPS are by menu or with the Shredder.

USING MENU TO DELETE

1. To delete an object, click button 2 on it to display its pop-up menu. One of the menu choices is Delete.

2. When you click on it, the Delete Object(s) dialog box appears. It gives you the opportunity to order the deletion by clicking on the Delete button, or if you have second thoughts, to cancel the delete operation.

3. If you have not changed the default confirmation before deletion, yet another dialog box asks you for confirmation.

4. Upon receiving confirmation, the WPS deletes the object.

Menu deletes will not work if the object is non-deletable or a copy of a non-deletable object. Some objects, such as the Master Help Index, are set as NODELETE at install time.

 Don't make copies of non-deletable objects. You will have a hard time getting rid of them.

It is possible to delete non-deletable objects, although WPS does not provide the ability. Gregory Czaja's freeware program named Black Hole, available on CompuServe's OS/2 Developer Forum 1 will destroy just about anything. Browse library 3 with a search key of BL*.* to find the latest version of it. After you install Black Hole, its icon appears on your desktop. Anything you drop into the Black Hole is gone forever. (Unless you can catch it before it hits the event horizon. See discussion of UNDELETE later in this chapter.)

 The Black Hole can get you into trouble. If you drop something essential to OS/2's operation into it, you could make your system inoperable. Use it with extreme care. It might be wise to hide the Hole in an obscure folder.

USING SHREDDER TO DELETE

When you want to delete an object, it is fairly easy to open its pop-up menu, select Delete and make the appropriate confirmations. However, it is even easier to just drag the object to the Shredder object and drop it in. Some types of objects will disappear right away. Others will ask for a couple of confirmations before disappearing.

 Some objects cannot be easily removed with the Shredder. Templates, for example, cannot be shredded.

Uncheck the Template property in its Settings notebook to render any template shreddable.

A difference between the menu method of deletion and the Shredder method is that templates can be deleted via their pop-up menus, after several confirmations. The Black Hole, of course, gobbles up templates just like everything else.

Recovering Deleted Objects

Inevitably, there will be times when you delete something and later discover that you need it after all. OS/2 provides for this common problem, but not through the Workplace Shell. To use OS/2's UN-DELETE facility, you must use one of the full screen or windowed command prompts.

When UNDELETE is active, nothing really gets deleted. When OS/2 receives a delete command from you or from the WPS, rather than deleting the files, it just renames them and copies them into the DELETE directory. The DELETE directory is a first-in-first-out buffer. When it fills up, the next deletion pushes out the oldest (and thus least likely to be needed again) deleted file or files and replaces them with the new ones. As long as you UNDELETE a deleted file before it has been pushed out of the DELETE directory, you can recover it.

OS/2 does not set up the Undelete function automatically. Provision for it must be made both in the CONFIG.SYS and the AUTOEXEC.BAT files. CONFIG.SYS must contain a statement similar to the following:

```
SET DELDIR=C:\DELETE,512;D:\DELETE,512;E:\DELETE,512;
```

AUTOEXEC.BAT should have:

```
SET DELDIR=C:\DELETE,512;D:\DELETE,512;E:\DELETE,512;
```

These statements establish delete directories 512 KB in size on each of three disk drives. Your statements may vary depending on your hardware configuration.

By default, UNDELETE is not enabled during a normal installation. Instead, the commands shown above are preceded by REM in both CONFIG.SYS and AUTOEXEC.BAT. REM (standing for remark), telling the command interpreter to ignore the rest of the line. This process, called "REMming out" a command is a common method of disabling a command that you may want to reinstate later.

If you want to use UNDELETE, remove the REM from the SET DELDIR commands in CONFIG.SYS and AUTOEXEC.BAT.

If you enable the SET DELDIR commands, you must be sure that you can spare the disk space that they require. It will be unavailable for your normal storage needs.

To use UNDELETE, you must be in the directory from which the file you want was deleted, or specify the full path. Move to that directory before issuing a command in the form:

```
UNDELETE filename.ext
```

If you want to undelete several related files from a directory, use wildcards such as:

```
UNDELETE YEAR199?.WQ1
```

UNDELETE takes several parameters. To undelete all recently deleted files from the current (or specified) directory use /S.

```
UNDELETE /S
```

The /A parameter recovers all deleted files if they are still present in the DELETE directory, without prompting for confirmation on each one. The /F parameter removes files from the DELETE directory so they cannot be recovered. The /L parameter lists files that are available for undeletion, without recovering them.

 UNDELETE recovers files that were deleted with the DEL or the ERASE command from either the OS/2 or the DOS prompt. It also recovers files deleted by selecting Delete on the file object's pop-up menu, and those deleted by dropping them into the Shredder. It even undeletes file objects dropped into the Black Hole.

Copying, Moving & Deleting Multiple Selected Objects

Earlier in this chapter we discussed the various methods of selecting multiple objects. Once a multiple selection has been made, the entire group can be copied, moved or deleted in a single operation.

Use the same actions that you would use to move, copy or delete a single object. If you are dragging with your mouse, multiple images of the icons in the group will travel under the mouse pointer. When you have finished, all objects in the group will have been moved, copied or deleted, as appropriate.

Renaming Selected Objects

You can change the name of any object on the desktop by calling up its Settings notebook. On the General page, in the Title box, change the name. This will change not only the name that appears on the desktop, but, if applicable, the name of the underlying file as well.

The Clipboard

The clipboard is one of OS/2's most valuable tools. With it you can transfer text or a graphical image from one application to another. Transfers can be across environments, with the source or destination being OS/2, WIN-OS/2 or DOS.

If you are already familiar with the Windows clipboard, then you know how the OS/2 clipboard works too. Both tools work the same way. The clipboard is used by applications rather than by the WPS itself. It is a temporary storage area where an application can stash a piece of text or a graphic. Since the clipboard functions outside of the application, it can relocate the stashed material to a different application as well as to a different location in the original application.

There are four clipboard operations: mark, cut, copy and paste. The source application must have some way of *marking* the material to be transferred to the clipboard. For text this usually involves selecting it with the mouse. For graphics draw a box around it with the mouse.

Once marked, you can either cut or copy the selected material. When you *cut*, the selected material is placed on the clipboard and removed from its original location. When you *copy*, the selected material is copied to the clipboard and left in its original location.

Once the clipboard contains the desired material, open the target application and place the cursor at the spot you want to insert it. Select the application's *paste* function to transfer the contents of the clipboard to the cursor location.

Using the clipboard to copy material from one part of an OS/2 application to another part of the same application involves a straightforward application of mark, cut (or copy) and paste. Transporting material from one OS/2 application to another is only a little more complicated. You could have both source and destination applications open and visible on the desktop at the same time.

Keep the Clipboard Viewer open and minimized. The Clipboard Viewer is one of the applets in the Productivity folder. It displays whatever is currently stored on the OS/2 clipboard. When minimized, it will be easily accessible but not take up valuable desktop space.

COPY FROM A WINDOWS APPLICATION TO AN OS/2 APPLICATION

Transporting material from a Windows application running under WIN-OS/2 to an OS/2 application, or vice versa, is somewhat more complex. Both OS/2 and WIN-OS/2 have clipboards. By default these clipboards are synchronized with each other, or *public*. When the clipboards are public, anything saved on one of them simultaneously appears on the other. This configuration is particularly valuable when you have migrated Windows applications to the OS/2 desktop. They can exchange data with your OS/2 applications as if they were OS/2 applications.

If you want to maintain two separate clipboards and not exchange information between them, you can set them to *private*. Use the Settings notebook for the WIN-OS/2 Setup object in the System Setup folder. Select the Data Exchange tab, displaying the page shown in Figure 4-14. Click on the appropriate radio button, then exit the Settings notebook. From this point on, the two clipboards will no longer share information.

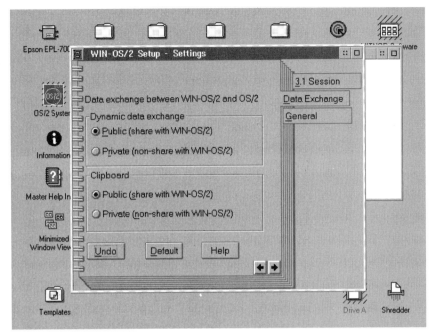

Figure 4-14: The Settings page for Clipboard and Dynamic Data Exchange.

Dynamic Data Exchange

The second data exchange mechanism shown on the WIN-OS/2 Setup Settings notebook (Figure 4-14) is Dynamic Data Exchange (DDE). Whereas with the clipboard you can exchange such static objects as blocks of text, graphical bitmaps and metafiles, DDE goes further. If two files or sessions are connected by a DDE link, changes made to one are immediately reflected in the other.

If you start two OS/2 sessions, each running its own application, the two applications can share data, either immediately with a "hot link" or upon request with a "warm link." As soon as you enter data into a field of one application, the same data appears in the corresponding field of the application hot-linked to it.

When your DDE link is set to public, you can instantaneously exchange data between an OS/2 application and a WIN-OS/2 application. If the DDE link is set to private, you can DDE-link one OS/2 application to another OS/2 application, or one WIN-OS/2 application to another WIN-OS/2 application, but you cannot create such a link between an OS/2 application and a WIN-OS/2 application.

THE DESKTOP NAVIGATION KEYS

We have mentioned several times that every effect that can be caused by a mouse action can also be achieved from the keyboard. Table 4-1 is a comprehensive list of operations and the key combinations that produce them.

Table 4-1. Keyboard control of the Workplace Shell.

WINDOW TASKS	
Operation	**Keys**
Get Help	F1
Display the Window List	Ctrl+Esc
Switch to the next window	Alt+Tab
Switch to the next window or full-screen session	Alt+Esc
Display window's pop-up menu	Alt+Spacebar
Move a window	Alt+F7, arrow keys
Size a window	Alt+F8, arrow keys
Set window default size	Alt,S, arrow keys,Enter
Minimize a window	Alt+F9
Hide a window	Alt+F11
Maximize a window	Alt+F10
Close a window	Alt+F4
Move up through contents of a window a page at a time	Page Up
Move down through contents of a window a page at a time	Page Down
Move to and from the window's menu bar	F10

OBJECT TASKS

Operation	Keys
Get Help	F1
Move among objects	arrow keys
Select an object	space bar
Select multiple objects	Shift+F8,arrow keys, spacebar. Repeat. Shift+F8 to end.
Select all objects in window	Shift+/
Deselect all objects in window	Shift+\
Open the selected object	Enter
Delete the selected object	Shift+F10,select Delete
Print the selected object	Shift+F10,select Print
Move the selected object	Shift+F10,select Move
Copy the selected object	Shift+F10,select Copy
Rename the selected object	Shift+F10,Right arrow, Enter,select General tab, select Title field, edit name.
Display desktop's pop-up menu	Alt+Shift+Tab,Ctrl+\, Shift+F10
Display selected object's pop-up menu	Shift+F10
Select first choice on pop-up menu	Home
Select last choice on pop-up menu	End
Menu choice "hot key" accelerator	Type underlined letter
Toggle between object and Help window	Alt+F6

NOTEBOOK TASKS	
Operation	**Keys**
Get Help	F1
Move to next page	Alt+Page Down
Move to previous page	Alt+Page Up
Move cursor from notebook page to tab	Alt+Up arrow
Move cursor from tab to notebook page	Alt+Down arrow
Move to next field on notebook page	Tab
Move to next item within a field	Arrow keys
Select an item in a single selection field	Enter
Select an item in a multiple selection field	Spacebar

 One way to switch quickly from one application window to another is to press Alt+Tab until the window you want comes to the top. This will work even if it is covered by other windows.

 If you want to switch to a full-screen session or a minimized session, press Alt+Esc instead.

 An even faster way to switch sessions is to press Ctrl+Esc to display the Window List, then select the desired session.

MOVING ON

In this chapter we have seen how the appearance and actions of the objects on the desktop are controlled by their Settings notebooks. We have also discussed some of the less commonplace desktop objects and how they can make your job easier. The UNDELETE facility can save your fanny. DDE data sharing can save you many hours of tedious file processing. Speaking of file processing, the next chapter reveals some potential problems that can be very dangerous to your data's health, along with some potions that should defeat the dangers and keep your files fit.

Chapter 5

FILE MAGIC

The Workplace Shell is the virtual world that you see represented on your computer screen. A collection of files residing on disk drives is the reality that lies underneath. All the data held by your computer and all the application programs that provide access to that data exist as disk files. The WPS allows users to deal with files without having to fully understand them.

THE DRIVES OBJECT

The Drives object in the OS/2 System folder gives access to all the files on your system stored on the drives. Drives may be floppy disks, hard disks, CD-ROM drives, optical drives or write once read many (WORM) drives. When you double-click on the Drives icon, one of three views of your drives is displayed: icon, tree or details. The default is Icon view (Figure 5-1).

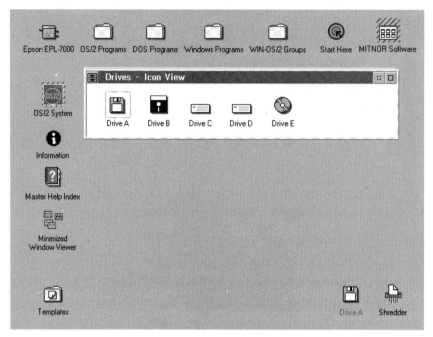

Figure 5-1: Icon view of drives on a typical system.

Icon View

Icon view displays an icon for each drive on the system. Figure 5-1 shows that drives A and B are floppy disk drives, drives C and D are hard disk drives and drive E is a CD-ROM drive. The icon for drive B is not a stock icon but one the author created to distinguish a 5.25-inch drive from the 3.5-inch drive A.

Icon view is the simplest, most Spartan view available. All it does is show you what drives you have. If you open one of the drives, it will display the folders and files it contains in either icon, tree or details view. Figure 5-2 shows that drive D has five subdirectories represented by folders. The fact that no file icons are displayed means that there are no files in drive D's root directory.

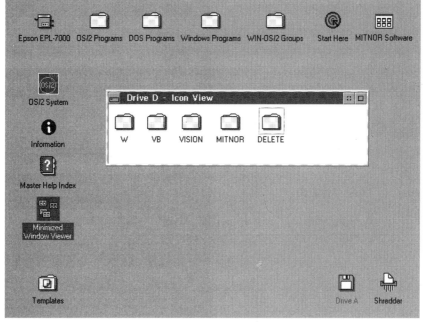

Figure 5-2: Icon view of drive D.

Tree View

Tree view of the system's disk drives tells more than Icon view does. In addition to showing what disks you have, it also displays what they contain. To show the Drives object's Tree view, click button 2 on the Drives icon in the OS/2 System window. Select Open, then choose Tree view. A fully collapsed tree view of your drives will be displayed, as shown in Figure 5-3. It does not show any details about what each drive contains. It does show that each drive is hierarchically subordinate to the Drives object.

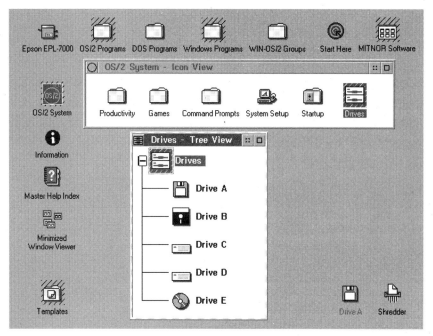

Figure 5-3: Fully collapsed Tree view of drive D.

To see more detail, double-click button 1 on one of the drive icons. A window will appear, probably in Icon view, showing folders and possibly files. The folders represent subdirectories of the drive's root directory. File icons (if any) represent files that are in the drive's root directory. A plus sign in a box will appear to the left of the drive icon you opened (Figure 5-4). This indicates that the drive D branch of the tree can be expanded.

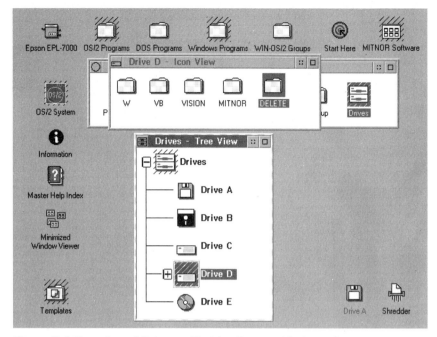

Figure 5-4: Tree view of Drives, with drive D opened in Icon view.

You can get a tree view of the contents of drive D by clicking button 1 on the plus sign. Figure 5-5 shows the result. The expanded tree does not fit in the window. You can expand the size of the window, but that only helps up to a point.

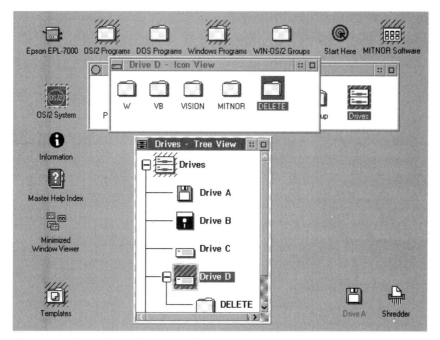

Figure 5-5: Tree view of Drives, with drive D branch expanded.

Change from normal size icons to small icons to show more of the tree. The Settings notebook for the Drives object lets you change Tree view to display either normal icons, small icons or no icons. This is true for a tree view of anything.

To change to small icons, click button 2 on the Drives object, select Open and Settings and move to page 2 of the View tab. This page controls the appearance of Tree view. Click the Small size radio button. Your tree view of the Drives object will become more compact, revealing much more of the structure.

Figure 5-6 shows that drive D has five subdirectories named DELETE, W, MITNOR, VB and VISION. Plus signs indicate that the VB and VISION subdirectories have subdirectories of their own.

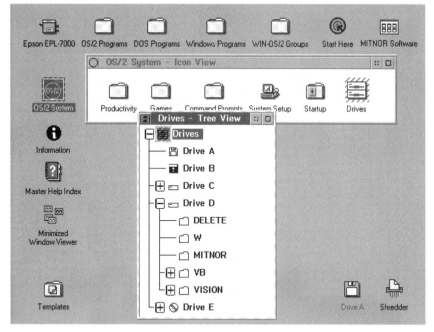

Figure 5-6: Small icon view reveals more of directory tree.

You can keep clicking on plus signs until you reach the lowest level subdirectory down any branch of the directory tree. Tree view does not show files, however, only directories (folders). A *folder* is a desktop object that represents a directory on a physical disk drive.

Details View

To see what files are in a directory and learn some basic facts about them, use Details view. From the pop-up menu for the folder you want to examine, select Open then Details view (Figure 5-7).

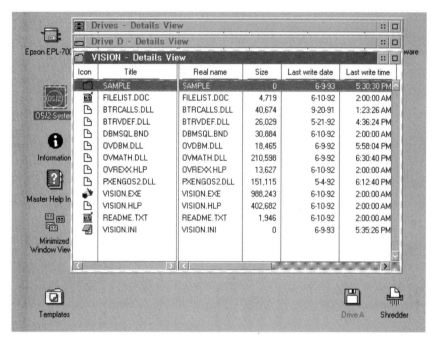

Figure 5-7: Details view of VISIONS subdirectory.

In this example, the VISIONS directory has a subdirectory named SAMPLE and a number of files. The view shows each file or directory's icon, its title, real name, size, last write date, last write time, last access date, last access time, creation date, creation time and the state of the file's flags.

Depending on how much you want to know about a file system, you can use Icon view, Tree view and Details view or any combination of them to determine the structure and content of your disks.

MANIPULATING FILES

Manipulating objects on the desktop, as discussed in Chapter 4, "The Workplace Shell," corresponds to manipulating files on disks. There are just a few important facts to remember.

1. Folders on the desktop represent directories on one of your system's disk drives.

2. File objects, shown as icons on the desktop, represent program files or data files on one of your system's disk drives.

3. By manipulating objects on the desktop you are affecting files on the disk drives.

Moving Files

After selecting one or more file icons, you can drag them from one folder to another. The underlying file or files will be copied to the destination drive/directory and deleted from the source drive/directory. During the move, exact copies of the icons follow the mouse pointer from the source to the destination.

 Dragging a file icon to the Shredder and dropping it in deletes it from its original location without copying it to a new location. This is not true, however, if UNDELETE is enabled. (See discussion in Chapter 4.)

 When you drag a file object to a floppy disk object, the file is copied rather than moved. After the operation is complete you have two copies of the file, your original and a new copy on the floppy. This is a safety feature, since people often want to back up files to floppy without removing them from the hard disk.

 Dragging a file icon from a floppy disk to the desktop also copies rather than moves the underlying file.

 If you want to archive a group of files to floppy and remove them from your hard disk, use Shift+mouse button 2 to override the default and force the move.

Copying Files

Copying files from the Workplace Shell is similar to moving them. To perform copies, hold the Ctrl key down while dragging file icons. The underlying files will be copied rather than moved.

When you Ctrl+drag a file icon located in a folder on a hard disk to another folder on the same or another hard disk, the underlying file is copied and ends up in both places.

When you Ctrl+drag a file icon to the Shredder, you receive the "Do Not Enter" sign, meaning that you cannot copy a file to the Shredder. Such an operation would be meaningless. Rather than making a copy and then immediately destroying it, OS/2 refuses to do anything.

 When you Ctrl+drag a file icon to the Drive A object, your file is copied to the floppy. This is exactly the same thing that happens when you do a simple drag to the Drive A object. If you keep in mind that Ctrl+drag *means* copy, you can't go wrong.

Shadowing Files

Shadow objects on the desktop do not bear a one-to-one relationship with files on disk, as file objects do.

When you move or delete a shadow, the original file object icon and the file it represents are unaffected.

When you move an original object icon, its shadow is unaffected but when you delete the original object icon, its shadow disappears at the same time.

If an original object icon is on removable media, such as a floppy disk or removable hard disk, and you physically replace that media with another disk, the object's shadows become "ghosts." The shadows will not function, because they have lost their connection to the real file. However, they will not disappear either.

Whenever you remove a floppy, removable hard or optical disk from your system, close its drive object on the desktop. Re-open the drive object with a new floppy, hard or optical disk cartridge in place. OS/2 will read the disk's directory again, determine that the files on the original disk are no longer present and erase all their shadows from the desktop.

ASSOCIATING A FILE WITH AN APPLICATION

On your system are two main types of files: data files and the applications that use them. In many cases a particular data file will normally, and sometimes only, be used by one application. It is convenient for those files to be *associated* with the application that uses them. Without associations you have to perform two operations every time you want to work on a data file. First you have to open the application that uses it. Then you have to open the data file itself.

 When a data file is associated with an application, all you have to do is double-click on the data file. This action prompts the application to load first, followed by the data file. After this one action, you can start work on the file.

Some associations are already set up by default. For instance, if you open the icon for a text file, the System Editor will automatically be launched and the text file placed in its workspace. If you double-click on an icon with an .ICO extension, the Icon Editor will be started and your icon will be loaded into its workspace. If you open the icon for a migrated Windows Write (.WRI) file, Windows Write will be launched first, then the file.

 You can create your own associations. You can associate all files of a particular type with an application, all files with a particular extension (such as .ICO or .WRI) or all files with similar filenames.

You can form another kind of association for data files that may be used by several applications. Instead of starting one application automatically, you can add several to the data file's pop-up menu. Then you can choose the application you want to load with the data file.

Associating by File Type or Filename

Establish an association by file type or filename from the application's Settings notebook. For example, look at the Association tab of the Settings notebook of the OS/2 System Editor (Figure 5-8).

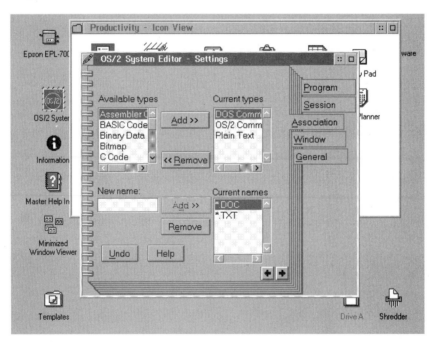

Figure 5-8: Association by type or name.

In the upper left are all the available file types. In the upper right are the three types currently associated with the System Editor: DOS command files, OS/2 command files and plain text files. If you double-click on a file that has any of these three types, the System Editor and the target file will be loaded.

In the lower right are the filenames currently associated with the System Editor. Any file that has an extension of .DOC or .TXT is associated. In the lower left you can enter a new filename to associate with the System Editor. If you want to associate more than one file, you can use wildcard characters in the name (as in *.DOC).

Associating From a Pop-up Menu

To associate a data file and an application from the file's pop-up menu, you must work with the file's Settings notebook rather than the application's. The procedure is significantly more complex.

1. Open the data file's Settings notebook and move to the Menu tab (Figure 5-9).

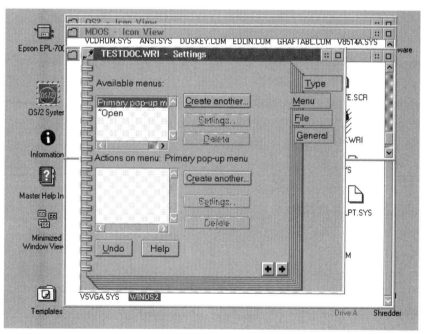

Figure 5-9: The data file Settings notebook, Menu tab.

2. From Available menus:, select ~Open. The tilde (~) before Open and Settings means that selections exist for these choices (Figure 5-10). Currently the example file is associated with Windows Write.

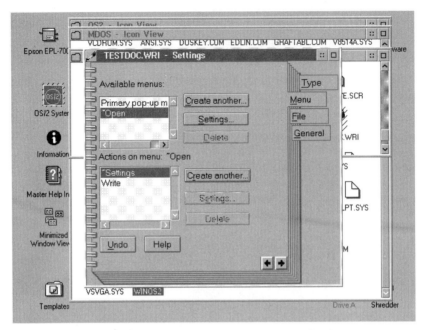

Figure 5-10: Actions on menu: ~Open displayed in lower list box.

3. Click on the *lower* Create another... button. The Menu Item Settings dialog box pops up (Figure 5-11).

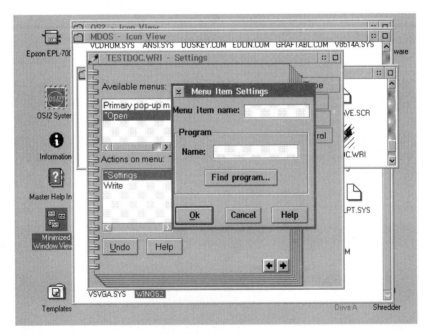

Figure 5-11: The Menu Item Settings dialog box.

4. Type in the name of the application you want to add to the menu. Type the name as you want it to appear in the Menu item name: box and the actual filename in the Program Name: box. Figure 5-12 shows the settings for our example. If you are unsure of the name, press the Find program... button to have OS/2 ask you what you know about the application. It will then search and display a list of all files that meet your criteria. Select the proper one from the list.

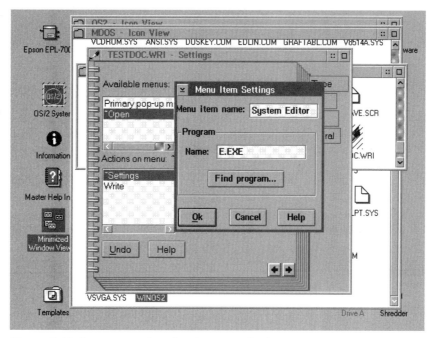

Figure 5-12: A new menu item has been specified.

5. Once you have added the new application close the Settings notebook.

Now when you click button 2 on the data file's icon and select Open from the pop-up menu, a submenu appears listing both the original associated application and the one you have just added (Figure 5-13). The check mark shows that Windows Write is still the default choice. If you double-click on the TESTDOC.WRI icon, it will still launch Windows Write. However, if you select System Editor from the menu, the editor will be launched instead.

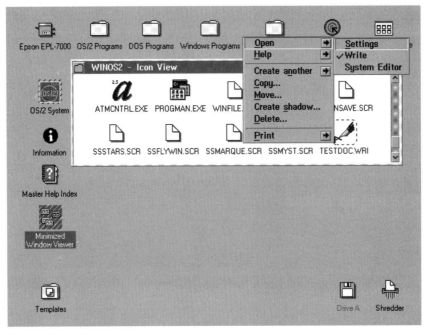

Figure 5-13: A new option has been added to data file's pop-up menu.

When you add a new application to a data file's pop-up menu, make sure it is compatible with the data in the file. In this example's case, the editor will issue a warning to the effect that the data file contains null characters. This is because Windows Write inserts non-ASCII control characters into its documents. The System Editor handles only ASCII characters correctly and ignores the non-ASCII characters. If all you want to do is read the text, the System Editor will do it. This can be a help when you want to read a text file but do not have the word processor that created it.

FINDING LOST FILES

With today's large hard disks and multi-level directory trees, it may be easy to lose track of a particular file. You may wonder whether the file you want is on the system at all. The Workplace Shell provides a couple of tools to help you either find misplaced files or tell you definitively that they do not exist. One tool is simple, powerful and easy to use but requires that you have some knowledge of filenames and disk drives. The other doesn't require any knowledge of hardware or physical file structure (which is good) but is not able to search for characters within a file (which is bad).

The Seek and Scan Files Applet

One of the little freebie applets in the Productivity folder, Seek and Scan Files, is a very valuable tool. It works like magic at finding lost files. In Chapter 3, "Getting Programs to Run," we described how to use it to find files you know by name or files that contain a particular character string. There is a small problem with using it, however.

To use the Seek and Scan Files applet, the user must be familiar with the real name of the desired file, not just its desktop title. It also helps to know which drive it might be on, so that time is not wasted checking large drives where it is unlikely to be.

In other words, the user must know something of the real world where disk files are stored, rather than just the virtual world of folders and icons. If you are comfortable dealing with drives, directories and possibly cryptic file names, this applet may be perfect for you.

The Find Tool

If you want to stick with the desktop metaphor and still find your misplaced files, you can do it with the Find tool, available from any folder's pop-up menu (Figure 5-14). There is only one page in the notebook, the one marked by the Include tab. On this page you specify what kinds of objects should be included in the search. The default search is the most general, which also means the most time consuming. Every object in the folder (and potentially all its subfolders, too) is examined to see if it matches the filename you have specified.

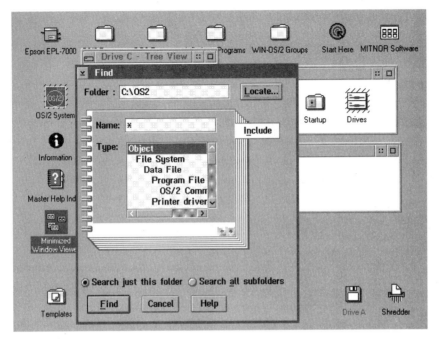

Figure 5-14: The Find notebook.

When using Find, it probably doesn't pay to try to narrow the search down to an exact file type. The search won't take more than a few seconds anyway, unless you are searching directories that contain many thousands of files.

Radio buttons near the bottom of the page allow you to specify whether only the current directory is searched or the current directory plus all of its subdirectories. The current directory is listed at the top of the page in the Folder: window.

If you click on the Locate... button it opens another notebook, this one with five tabs (Figure 5-15).

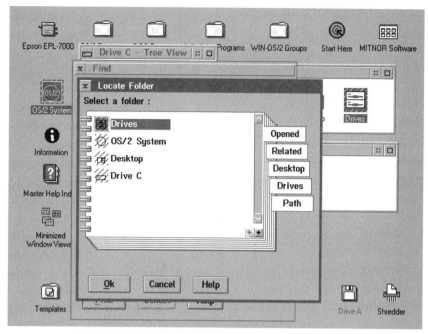

Figure 5-15: The Locate notebook within the Find notebook.

 The Locate function doesn't do much and is probably not worth bothering with. The Find function works fine without it.

PENETRATING INNER MYSTERIES

OS/2, like life itself, harbors mysteries that are not evident to the naked eye. Advanced practitioners of computer voodoo are well aware that in addition to the visible world that we can see, there is another, invisible world that exerts a powerful influence. You can learn the secrets of that invisible world and in so doing join an elite group of druids that grasps the reality behind the merely apparent.

Hidden Files

Files in the OS/2 file system (or DOS file system for that matter) may have *attributes* that set them apart in some way. One attribute is the *system* attribute. System files are essential to the operation of OS/2. If a system file is removed or altered in any way, OS/2 will probably not work at all. The *hidden* attribute is another one that applies to only a few select files. A hidden file, as the name implies, does not show up when you view a directory. The Workplace Shell does not reveal its presence when you ask for a Details view of the directory the hidden file is in.

Long Filenames

One of the big improvements of OS/2 over DOS is that you can give your files long filenames that really mean something. This helps a lot when you are trying to figure out what to do with a file that you created eight months ago. Under DOS you are allowed eight characters of filename and three characters of extension. That is all. It is hardly enough to say something meaningful about the file.

With OS/2 your filenames may be up to 254 characters. They may contain spaces, periods and other characters that are not legal in a DOS filename. How is this possible? OS/2 supports the file allocation table (FAT) directory structure that was developed for DOS. On a FAT-formatted OS/2 volume, both DOS and OS/2 files may co-exist. OS/2 is backward-compatible with DOS. If you give a file a long name, that name is translated into a unique label that fits within the DOS limits. The long file name and its equivalent DOS-compatible identifier are *extended attributes*. Extended attributes for a disk volume are kept by OS/2 in a hidden file in that volume's root directory.

Hidden files may not be deleted, moved or manipulated in any way. It is possible to "unhide" hidden files to make them visible in their directory and susceptible to manipulation. If, however, all you want to do is check whether they are present, there is an easier way.

When you open a full-screen (or windowed) OS/2 session, you can enter commands directly at the operating system's Command Prompt. To view the contents of a directory (the files in a folder), switch to that directory, then issue a DIR command. Figure 5-16 shows the contents of a directory named DELETE.

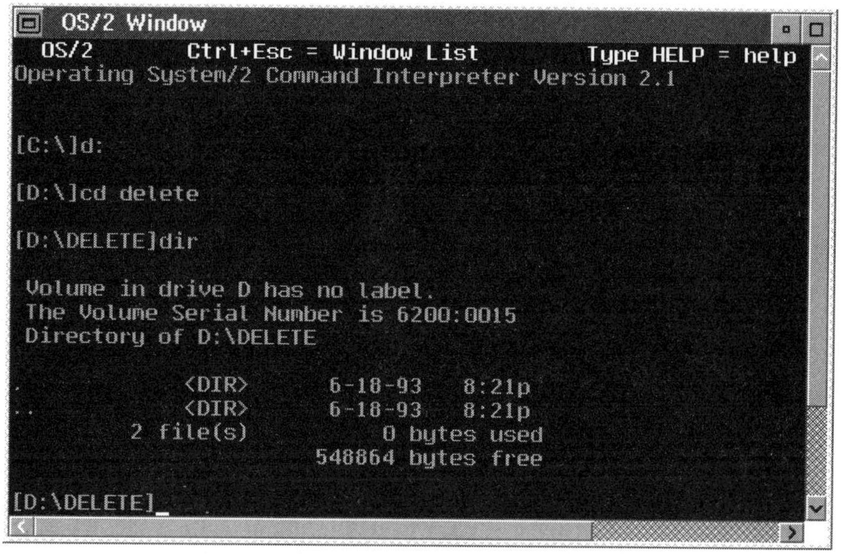

```
┌────────────────────────────────────────────────────────┐
│ ▣  OS/2 Window                                      ▫ □ │
│  OS/2        Ctrl+Esc = Window List      Type HELP = help│▲
│ Operating System/2 Command Interpreter Version 2.1      │
│                                                         │
│ [C:\]d:                                                 │
│                                                         │
│ [D:\]cd delete                                          │
│                                                         │
│ [D:\DELETE]dir                                          │
│                                                         │
│  Volume in drive D has no label.                        │
│  The Volume Serial Number is 6200:0015                  │
│  Directory of D:\DELETE                                 │
│                                                         │
│  .           <DIR>        6-18-93    8:21p              │
│  ..          <DIR>        6-18-93    8:21p              │
│         2 file(s)           0 bytes used               │
│                       548864 bytes free                │
│                                                         │
│ [D:\DELETE]_                                            │▼
└────────────────────────────────────────────────────────┘
```

Figure 5-16: A normal directory display of the DELETE folder.

The directory appears to be empty. The display claims that zero bytes are used. Hah! If you believe this, you are definitely not a voodoo master. There are hidden files here. To see them, you need only to add a parameter to the DIR command. Issue the command DIR /AH. Figure 5-17 shows the result.

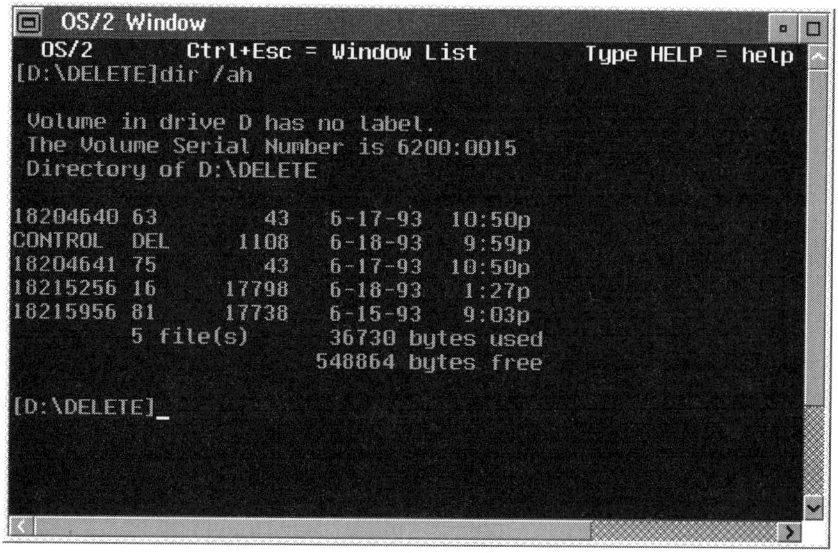

```
┌────────────────────────────────────────────────────────┐
│ ▣  OS/2 Window                                      ▫ □ │
│  OS/2        Ctrl+Esc = Window List      Type HELP = help│▲
│ [D:\DELETE]dir /ah                                      │
│                                                         │
│  Volume in drive D has no label.                        │
│  The Volume Serial Number is 6200:0015                  │
│  Directory of D:\DELETE                                 │
│                                                         │
│ 18204640 63          43     6-17-93   10:50p            │
│ CONTROL  DEL       1108     6-18-93    9:59p            │
│ 18204641 75          43     6-17-93   10:50p            │
│ 18215256 16       17798     6-18-93    1:27p            │
│ 18215956 81       17738     6-15-93    9:03p            │
│         5 file(s)         36730 bytes used             │
│                          548864 bytes free             │
│                                                         │
│ [D:\DELETE]_                                            │
│                                                         │▼
└────────────────────────────────────────────────────────┘
```

Figure 5-17: Directory of the DELETE folder with the /AH parameter.

This form of the DIR command displays *only* hidden files. There are five hidden files in this directory. As you can see, they take up 36,730 bytes of disk space rather than the zero originally reported. 36k isn't a lot, but hidden files can be much larger.

Examining Space Usage by Extended Attribute Files

The extended attributes of the files in a volume (logical drive) are kept in that volume's root directory. Since they are in a hidden file, you can't tell how much of your disk space is being consumed by extended attributes with a normal DIR command. You can, however, use the /AH parameter with the DIR command (Figure 5-18).

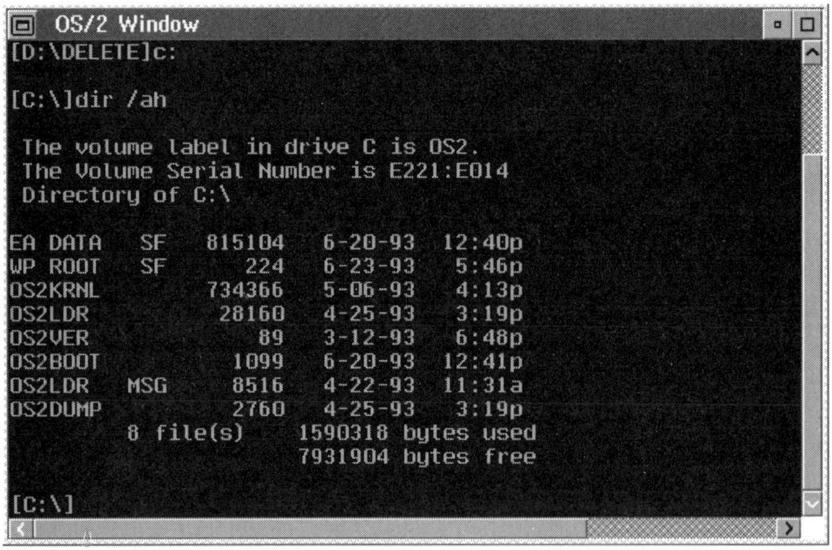

```
┌─────────────────────────────────────────────────────────────┐
│ □   OS/2 Window                                          ▫ □ │
│ [D:\DELETE]c:                                                │
│                                                              │
│ [C:\]dir /ah                                                 │
│                                                              │
│   The volume label in drive C is OS2.                        │
│   The Volume Serial Number is E221:E014                      │
│   Directory of C:\                                           │
│                                                              │
│ EA DATA   SF     815104   6-20-93   12:40p                   │
│ WP ROOT   SF        224   6-23-93    5:46p                   │
│ OS2KRNL         734366    5-06-93    4:13p                   │
│ OS2LDR           28160    4-25-93    3:19p                   │
│ OS2VER              89    3-12-93    6:48p                   │
│ OS2BOOT           1099    6-20-93   12:41p                   │
│ OS2LDR    MSG     8516    4-22-93   11:31a                   │
│ OS2DUMP           2760    4-25-93    3:19p                   │
│         8 file(s)     1590318 bytes used                     │
│                       7931904 bytes free                     │
│                                                              │
│ [C:\]                                                        │
└─────────────────────────────────────────────────────────────┘
```

Figure 5-18: Boot volume hidden files.

There are over 1.5 MB of hidden files in this directory. Besides being hidden, they are all system files and thus part of the operating system. OS2KRNL is a big one as you might expect. OS/2 is a complex operating system, so it is not surprising that its main component, or *kernel*, is large. Notice, however, that the biggest file is "EA DATA. SF." This is the file in which the extended attributes (EAs) are stored. The size of this file will change as files are added to and erased from the volume.

Unhiding system files then changing anything about them is very dangerous business. Don't do it unless you have everything fully backed up with OS/2-compatible backup software and you really know what you are doing.

   Attention Apprentice Magicians: Don't even *think* about touching this stuff.

   Now that I have warned you of the danger of unhiding and changing system files, I will tell you how to do it. I trust you to make only legitimate use of this knowledge and not to pass it on to anyone who is not ready for it.

   With the ATTRIB command you can change the attributes of any file. You can turn a system file into a non-system file or a hidden file into a non-hidden file. There are a couple of other attributes that you can reverse, but we are not concerned with them here.

 Never do this. To really expose your system to danger, issue the following command in the root directory of your boot volume:

```
ATTRIB -H -S *.*
```

   This command will remove the hidden attribute and the system attribute from all hidden and system files in the current directory. Once these files are exposed to the light of day they can easily be changed or even deleted. Once that happens, don't expect anything to work right.

Deleting Files From an Old DELETE Directory

Although it is extremely rare that even a voodoo master would have occasion to change the attributes of a system file, you may want to unhide certain hidden files that are not also system files. If a file is hidden but no longer needed, it is taking up valuable disk space. To delete it, you must first unhide it.

   Consider the files in the D:\DELETE directory shown in Figure 5-17. Let's say that some time in the past the UNDELETE feature was enabled on your system to allow you to recover deleted files.

Later, however, you decided the feature wasn't all that valuable and disabled it by turning the SET DELDIR statements into remarks in both your CONFIG.SYS and AUTOEXEC.BAT files. That alone does not recover the space occupied by the files that were deleted while UNDELETE was enabled. They are still there, although hidden in the DELETE directory. To get rid of those old deleted files and recover the space they are using, you must first unhide them, then (really) delete them.

To unhide files that are not system files, go to the directory where they are located and issue the following command:

```
ATTRIB -H *.*
```

Figure 5-19 shows the result. At the top of the screen is a directory that has not quite scrolled off. It shows no files and no bytes used. After the ATTRIB command has unhidden all hidden files, a new DIR command (with no parameters) shows the five formerly hidden files. Since UNDELETE is no longer enabled, you can now get rid of these files permanently with a simple DEL command.

```
DEL *.*
```

At this point, you can even remove the directory if you wish. It is no longer needed.

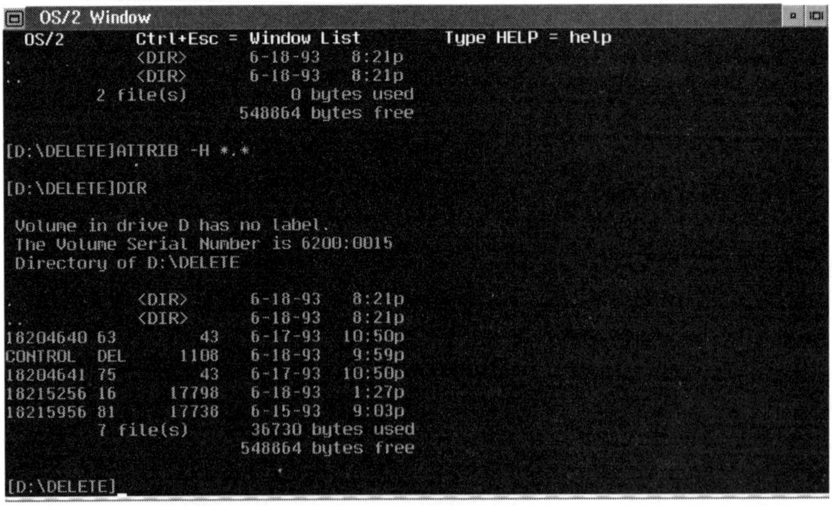

```
┌─□ OS/2 Window                                              □ |□|
  OS/2          Ctrl+Esc = Window List       Type HELP = help
      .          <DIR>         6-18-93    8:21p
      ..         <DIR>         6-18-93    8:21p
          2 file(s)            0 bytes used
                          548864 bytes free

[D:\DELETE]ATTRIB -H *.*

[D:\DELETE]DIR

 Volume in drive D has no label.
 The Volume Serial Number is 6200:0015
 Directory of D:\DELETE

      .          <DIR>         6-18-93    8:21p
      ..         <DIR>         6-18-93    8:21p
18204640 63           43       6-17-93   10:50p
CONTROL  DEL        1108       6-18-93    9:59p
18204641 75           43       6-17-93   10:50p
18215256 16        17798       6-18-93    1:27p
18215956 81        17738       6-15-93    9:03p
          7 file(s)        36730 bytes used
                          548864 bytes free

[D:\DELETE]
```

Figure 5-19: Unhide all files in the current directory.

FILE SYSTEMS, FAT vs. HPFS

OS/2 can operate with files that are organized according to two different file systems. They are DOS's venerable File Allocation Table (FAT) system and OS/2's newer High Performance File System (HPFS). You have a choice when you set up OS/2 initially to format your hard disk volumes according to either the FAT or the HPFS system. If you have multiple volumes, you can make some FAT volumes and others HPFS volumes. Within a volume, however, all files must be of the same type.

In general, most users are unaware of the distinction between FAT and HPFS volumes. If you copy a file from a FAT-formatted disk to a HPFS-formatted one by dragging an icon from one folder to another on the desktop, OS/2 transparently converts the file to the appropriate format on the target drive. You need not be concerned.

For many people an all-HPFS system is the best choice. HPFS handles long filenames naturally, whereas a OS/2 must translate them to short filenames for a FAT system. HPFS volumes are not subject to the dreaded fragmentation that will be discussed later in this chapter. Due to a number of design improvements, file access in a HPFS volume is intrinsically faster than with a FAT volume. The larger the disk, the greater the advantage of HPFS.

The main disadvantage of HPFS is that it is not backward compatible with any version of DOS or with OS/2 versions 1.0 and 1.1. If you want files to be usable by both OS/2 2.X and DOS (on a Dual Boot or a Boot Manager system), they must be on a FAT volume.

The HPFS file system is compatible with Microsoft Windows NT. If you put OS/2 2.X and Windows NT on the same machine, they could share a HPFS-formatted partition (see Chapter 8, "Installation Magic").

INITIALIZATION FILES (Messing with these is risky.)

At boot time, after the basic OS/2 operating system wakes up, a large number of customizations must be applied to it so that everything will work the way you have specified. Several command files turn a basic, plain-vanilla system into a custom environment optimized for your particular needs and preferences.

CONFIG.SYS

Anyone with more than a passing familiarity with DOS has heard of the CONFIG.SYS file. It loads the device drivers used by the operating system (either DOS or OS/2) to communicate with peripheral devices such as printers, disk drives, CD-ROM drives, mice and video boards. It also contains commands that tell the operating system where important files are located.

OS/2's CONFIG.SYS file has a lot in common with the corresponding file in a DOS system. It is just bigger. With more things to control, the OS/2 file typically has more command lines. In a Dual Boot system, both DOS and OS/2 use the same CONFIG.SYS file.

AUTOEXEC.BAT

Under DOS, AUTOEXEC.BAT is a sequence of programs that are run at boot time before control is turned over to the user. OS/2 itself does not use AUTOEXEC.BAT. However, OS/2 is capable of running one or more DOS sessions in addition to OS/2 sessions. As each one of those DOS sessions is launched, AUTOEXEC.BAT is run for it. After the last command in the AUTOEXEC.BAT file is executed, the DOS prompt appears on the screen. Since AUTOEXEC.BAT is used only by DOS sessions, it functions in exactly the same way that it would on a native DOS machine.

STARTUP.CMD

STARTUP.CMD is to OS/2 what AUTOEXEC.BAT is to DOS. It is a file containing a sequence of commands that are executed at boot

time, right after the last command in CONFIG.SYS. Since
STARTUP.CMD is optional, it will not be present unless someone
creates it and places it into the root directory of the boot disk.

**The STARTUP.CMD command file serves the same purpose as
the Startup folder that is normally located in the OS/2 System
folder.** Of the two, the Startup folder is probably the easier to use.

**STARTUP.CMD has one potential advantage over an equivalent
Startup folder.** You can arrange the commands in such a way
that you can guarantee the order in which they are executed. If you
put equivalent icons in the Startup folder, OS/2's multitasking capability may run some of them concurrently. In some cases this method
of execution may not give you the results you want.

To guarantee the order of execution of commands in a
STARTUP.CMD file, place them in the order you want and precede
all commands after the first one with the && symbol pair. &&
means that the preceding command must be completed successfully
before the next one is begun. In the Startup folder, there is no equivalent of the && symbol pair to control the flow of execution.

.INI Files

After the CONFIG.SYS, AUTOEXEC.BAT and STARTUP.CMD
files, there are additional files that initialize other aspects of OS/2 and
the applications that run under it. These initialization files have the
extension .INI. These files control the way their associated programs
operate and are displayed. The normal way of changing the contents
of an .INI file is by making alterations to the Settings notebook of its
associated desktop object. It is also possible to change the contents of
an .INI file directly using a third-party .INI file editor.

**Changing an .INI file directly with an .INI file editor can be
dangerous.** If you inadvertently violate the acceptable syntax of
the file or enter a wrong value, you could render the underlying program, or even OS/2 itself, inoperable.

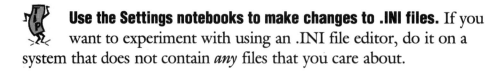

Use the Settings notebooks to make changes to .INI files. If you want to experiment with using an .INI file editor, do it on a system that does not contain *any* files that you care about.

DISK MAINTENANCE

OS/2 is a very big operating system and the many applications that run under it are even larger. Reliable hard disk storage is crucial to the functioning of OS/2. You cannot even boot the OS/2 desktop from floppy disk. Since a hard disk, like any other mechanical device, sometimes fails, there is a risk that you might lose all the data and programs stored on it. That data might be irreplaceable. You must have a way of creating backup copies and, when necessary, reloading them onto your system.

Backing Up

There are many excellent hard disk backup programs on the market for DOS systems. Unfortunately, most of them do not work for OS/2. Since DOS does not use extended attributes, backup programs written to run under DOS do not provide for saving them.

If you back up an HPFS file system created by OS/2 with a DOS file backup utility, it is likely that your files' extended attributes will not be saved. If this happens, you will have a mess when you restore. Your data will not be completely useless, but rebuilding it to its original state will be tedious and will require detailed knowledge of files.

There are third-party backup programs that support OS/2 extended attributes. Make sure a product supports OS/2 before you buy it. When you back up with a product that does not support OS/2, there will be no indication that anything is wrong. When you restore these files and you find something a bit odd about each one, it is too late to read the fine print on the backup software box.

Fragmenting & Defragmenting

Fragmentation is an unfortunate fact of life for any FAT-based file system. FAT-based file systems are a relic of the dim past, when the largest disk available for an IBM personal computer was 160 KB. Today a disk drive 1,000 times larger than that original IBM drive would be considered small. Disk fragmentation was not an issue at all at the beginning but is a major problem now.

Each track on a hard disk is divided into sectors. Sectors are typically 512 bytes in length, and one or more of them is grouped together into a cluster. A cluster is the smallest directly addressable unit on a hard disk. A disk's File Allocation Table contains an entry for every cluster on the disk.

As files are written to a disk they are assigned as many clusters as are needed to hold them. Initially the assignment of disk space is strictly sequential, using contiguous clusters. With the passage of time, some files are deleted, others remain and new ones are added. The new files fill up the holes left by the previously deleted files. Often the new file to be added is bigger than the first hole that is available to hold it. Consequently, some of the file is put into the first hole, some into the second and so on. With additional deletions and additions, the situation becomes progressively worse, until a newly stored file may be broken up into hundreds of chunks on the disk. Since it takes the disk read/write mechanism a significant amount of time to move from one chunk to the next, read and write operations slow down.

 A badly fragmented disk can be intolerably slow. If it seems file retrievals and writes are taking longer than they used to, and there has been a high rate of addition and deletion of files on your FAT-organized hard disk, it is probably becoming fragmented. To maintain reasonable performance, use a disk defragmenting utility on your hard disk, as needed.

If you have a DOS defragmenting utility that is not specifically designed to work under OS/2, exercise caution when using it.

DOS defragmenters will not handle extended attributes and other parts of the Workplace Shell properly. You must back these up first, run the defragmenter then restore the backed-up files. At this writing there is no native OS/2 FAT volume defragmenter available.

 Don't try to defragment your disk unless you have a procedure that you *know* works flawlessly with OS/2 FAT volumes. Log into the CompuServe OS2USER forum, find someone who seems to know what she is talking about and ask her what to do.

 To minimize the impact of fragmentation, make your OS/2 boot volume only big enough to hold OS/2. Do not put any other programs or data on that volume. Since you will never erase from or write to this volume after the initial installation, very little fragmentation will occur on it. Put all your programs and data on another volume. If this second volume uses HPFS, it will not become as fragmented. If it uses FAT, it may become fragmented, but you will be able to defragment it without worrying about extended attributes when a native OS/2 defragment utility becomes available.

MOVING ON

In this chapter we covered the real core of OS/2: the disk files. Aside from moving or copying files from one disk to another, you learned how to associate a data file to the applications that use it, how to find files buried somewhere on a large hard disk, how to bring hidden secrets to light and how to protect your files from destruction.

Knowledge of files is important for smooth and trouble-free operation. However, the real bottom line is results. If your system cannot translate your massive quantities of data into usable information and present it to you in an understandable form, what good is it? Presenting results in an understandable form usually involves creating printed reports. In the next chapter we will explore OS/2's printing capabilities, particularly looking at ways you can use them to go beyond the standard format report.

Chapter 6

CURSE-FREE PRINTING

I f there is any part of working with computers that might cause a temperate person to swear, it is printing. There are so many different things that can go wrong with the printing process that it seems a miracle whenever you get printed output that looks the way you want it to the first time.

You can increase the incidence of miracles dramatically by understanding the intricacies of OS/2's printing system as well as of your own hardware.

PREPARATION—GETTING READY TO PRINT

Let's assume that you have an operational OS/2 2.X system and a working printer is connected to it. Somewhere on your desktop, there should be an icon for the Printer object (Figure 6-1). The printer icon will look different if you have a dot-matrix printer.

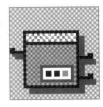

Figure 6-1: The Printer object icon.

An OS/2 system can have multiple printer objects, each with its own icon. A printer object icon does not necessarily correspond to a single printer, although usually that is the case. Instead it corresponds to a *print queue*, which is a sequence of print jobs waiting to be printed. Print queues feed into the *spooler*, which stores the jobs and arbitrates among jobs coming in from multiple queues.

The printer object pop-up menu (Figure 6-2) has two unique options, Change status and Set default. Change status has a submenu, as indicated by the arrow on the right edge of the menu. The two choices on the submenu are Hold and Release. When the Release option is in effect (the default), all jobs placed in the print queue are released immediately to the spooler (or if the spooler is disabled, directly to the printer). The assumption is that if you ask OS/2 to print something, you want the printed output as soon as possible.

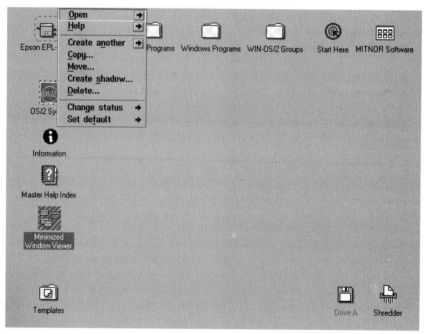

Figure 6-2: Printer object pop-up menu.

If you select the Hold option, however, print jobs placed in the queue will be held until you release them. There are several reasons why you might do this. For example, you might have run out of printer paper. You can keep working and adding jobs to the print queue while someone runs down to the office supply store. You can then release all pending jobs when he returns with the paper. Performance is another reason for selecting Hold. Although an OS/2 computer does not cease other processing while it is printing, it does slow down. You may want to schedule the printing for a later time when interactive use is lighter.

Adding a printer to a system can be a pretty involved process using Selective Install from the System Setup folder. If you are installing from floppy disk, a considerable amount of disk swapping might be needed. There is a much easier way.

 If you are adding a printer to your system, use the Printer template in the Templates folder. Follow this procedure:

1. Click button 2 on the Printer template in the Templates folder.

2. Select Install from the pop-up menu. The Create a Printer dialog box will appear (Figure 6-3). In this example, the box on the left shows that two printer drivers are already installed, one for an Epson EPL-7000 running in LaserJet emulation mode and another for the IBMNULL device. The IBMNULL device is a generic printer driver that will work with just about any printer, but will not support formatting (such as bold or italic type).

   On the right in Figure 6-3, icons for three parallel and four serial ports are shown. Diagonal lines in the background show that LPT1 is already in use by the EPL-7000. The dark background around the LPT2 icon means that OS/2 suggests you connect the new printer to LPT2.

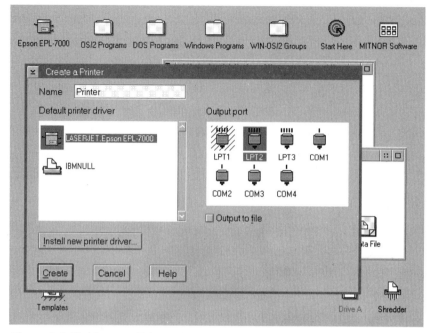

Figure 6-3: The Create a Printer dialog box.

3. The default name for your new printer is "Printer." This is not very descriptive. Enter a more appropriate name in the box at the top left.

4. Click on the Install new printer driver button. A dialog box will appear with a list of printer drivers. Most popular printers and quite a few obscure ones are supported by drivers shipped with OS/2.

5. Scroll through the list of supported printers. If your printer or a printer that your printer can emulate is listed, select it, then click on the Install button.

6. OS/2 will now install the new printer driver. If you have the OS/2 installation CD-ROM on line, a click on the OK button will copy the driver to your hard disk. If you install from floppies, you will be prompted to insert the appropriate floppy disks.

7. Once you have successfully installed the driver, click on the Create button at the bottom left of the Create a Printer dialog box. OS/2 will create the printer object then ask you if you want to install an equivalent WIN-OS/2 printer configuration.

8. Click on Yes if you plan to print anything on the new printer from WIN-OS/2.

 Use the IBMNULL printer driver if nothing else works and you need to output plain text.

 Since the IBMNULL printer driver has no frills, it is faster than any other driver you might try. Use it if raw speed is more important to you than formatting.

Each port you use requires a port address and an interrupt request line. If you have several devices such as a modem, a sound card, a network card or a SCSI adapter, there may be no interrupt request lines (IRQ) left for a second printer.

You can put two (or even more) printers on the same parallel port and switch between them with an inexpensive external printer switch. The problem with this approach is that you must make sure that you never have jobs going to both devices at the same time. If you decide to use an external printer switch, click on the LPT1 icon. Jobs slated for the new printer and the existing one will both be sent to port LPT1.

If your printer is not supported by a driver on the OS/2 install disks, you will have to get it from somewhere else. Likely sources of drivers are the manufacturer of your printer and the CompuServe OS2USER forum.

When you return to the desktop, you will see a new printer icon, representing your new printer.

> **Two printers can be in operation simultaneously.** If you have two printers connected to two different ports, you can send print jobs to both without worrying about possible conflicts.

> **If two printers are connected to the same port, make sure the port is switched to the proper printer before sending a print job to it.** If a document is formatted for one printer but sent to another, the output is likely to be garbled.

EXECUTION–PRINTING IN ACTION

Although OS/2 provides the means for printing, it does not print anything itself. Print jobs must be originated by applications running under OS/2 or WIN-OS/2, by icon dragging on the desktop or by OS/2 or DOS command prompts.

Printing From an OS/2 or WIN-OS/2 Menu

Print from an application under OS/2 may vary from one application to the next. Applications that are Workplace Shell-aware, WIN-OS/2 applications and DOS applications represent three different categories. Typically WPS-aware and WIN-OS/2 applications will have a pull-down menu named File. WPS-aware applications will have a Printer Setup option. Figure 6-4 shows the dialog box that appears when the printer selected is a LaserJet-compatible Epson EPL-7000 and the program calling it is PM Chart.

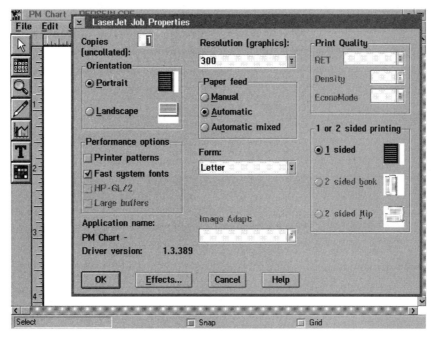

Figure 6-4: The printer setup dialog box for a laser printer.

This choice, if available, offers you considerable flexibility in specifying the properties of your printed output. You can set the number of copies, orientation, resolution and several other properties. When everything is the way you want it, press the OK button. Then select Print from the File menu. A submenu gives you a choice of Page, View and All pages.

If the text or graphics you want to print take up only a fraction of the page, select View. After you trace out a selection rectangle with your mouse, the subject will be expanded and centered to fill the page.

Many applications will offer a simple Print command without any options. Generally the applications that offer more print options are graphics, desktop publishing or high-level word processing applications for which quality printed output is essential.

Printing from an application running under WIN-OS/2 is similar to printing from a native OS/2 application. Print is generally an option under the File menu, but setup conventions follow the Windows model rather than the OS/2 standard.

Dragging a Document to the Printer Icon

Another way to print a document is to drag its icon to the printer object and drop it. It will immediately be sent to the printer (or spooler, if it is enabled).

Icon dragging only works for printing ASCII text files or print-ready files. Graphics or formatted files, however, will probably not print as you expect.

The PRINT Command

Although it is more common to print from an application, it is possible to print directly from OS/2 using the PRINT command at the OS/2 command prompt or at the DOS prompt. You can also use the PRINT command to cancel the printing of the current job as well as jobs waiting in the print queue.

The PRINT command is handy if you know the name of the file you want to print and you know what directory it is in. Drop to the command prompt, issue the command, then move on to other things as the spooler takes over responsibility for the print job.

As is the case with icon dropping, if you try to print anything other than an ASCII file or a print file, OS/2's Print Manager will not know what to do with it. The result may be a thick sheaf of garbage pages.

Printing to a File

You may occasionally need to create a print image on disk rather than on paper. If you are creating a series of images in quick succession, you can write them more quickly to disk than you can to most printers. You may want to print (or plot) images to a device that is not connected to your computer. When you output the images to disk, you can transport them by floppy or modem to a computer that has the desired output device.

Follow this procedure to print to a file:

1. Open your Printer object's Settings notebook.

2. Select the Printer driver tab.

3. Select the Printer driver for the target printer.

4. Select the Output tab.

5. Click on the Output to file box.

6. Select the Queue options tab.

7. Select Printer-specific format.

8. Close the Settings notebook.

9. Perform the print operation as you normally would. You will be prompted to enter a name for the output file.

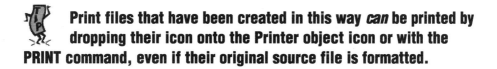 **Print files that have been created in this way *can* be printed by dropping their icon onto the Printer object icon or with the PRINT command, even if their original source file is formatted.**

Spooling & the Print Queue

The spooler can accept print jobs from multiple queues, store them on disk and print them in an orderly manner. It will keep everything separate, even when multiple print requests are made at the same time.

You can speed up printing by disabling the spooler. Spooling is an extra step and takes time. If you disable the spooler, however, you must make sure that you do not send the printer two different print jobs at the same time. Without the spooler to arbitrate, your printout may contain a mixture of both jobs rather than two separate documents.

Setting Priority to Speed Up Print Time

Your computer has a certain amount of processing capacity. You can choose to spend all of it on printing and none on processing other sessions, all on processing other sessions and none on printing, or some mix of the two.

In the Spooler Settings notebook, you can specify the print priority. There is a slide switch used to set print priority as low as 0 or as high as 189 (Figure 6-5). The default value is right in the middle at 95. The higher you set the priority, the faster the spooler will process your print jobs. It will rob CPU cycles from your other active sessions (if any), which will slow them down accordingly.

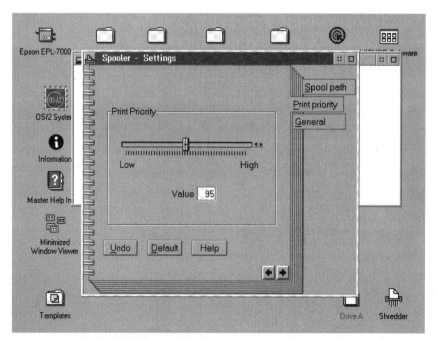

Figure 6-5: The Print Priority page in the Spooler Settings notebook.

Adjust print priority to match the way you work. When some people print, they don't care about anything else. They want their printout and they want it now! Such people should set print priority high. Others want to keep working at top speed, with the printing happening in the background and finishing whenever it finishes. They will look at the output later. These people should set print priority lower.

Printing the Screen

Some application output is specifically designed to be delivered in printed form and other output is designed to be viewed only on the screen. There are times, however, when you will want a permanent record of something that appears on the screen. Screen images are ephemeral—when you close an application or turn off your computer, the screen image is gone. You may find it difficult to duplicate the image at a later time or convince your friends that you really saw what you saw.

For example, say you are playing a little Reversi from the Games folder while you are waiting for a large print job to complete. You are playing at the Master level and you realize that you are boxing your opponent (the computer) in; the noose is drawing tighter and tighter. Usually the computer utterly destroys you at this level, but this time you have soundly trounced the Master! Terrific! You cannot, however, remember the exact sequence of moves that brought you to this point. You may never be able to reproduce this result. What can you do to make your friends believe you? Easy. Just press the Print Screen key on your keyboard. A printed image of your victory (Figure 6-6) will emerge from your printer and soon take up an honored place above the mantel in your living room.

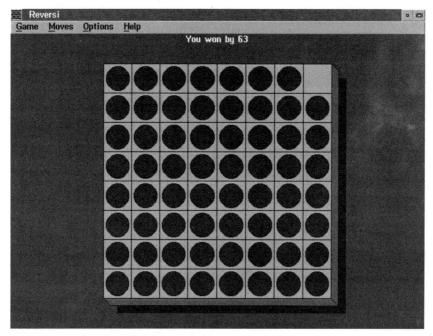

Figure 6-6: A permanent record of a Reversi triumph.

 A printed image of your victory will emerge only if Print Screen is enabled.

 You can still use Print Screen to bear testimony to your success, even if it was not enabled when you started your game.
Here is one instance where OS/2's multitasking comes to your rescue. Just minimize your Reversi window to get back to the desktop. Then open the Settings notebook for the System object in the System Setup folder. One of the pages, labeled Print Screen, has two options: Enable and Disable (Figure 6-7). Click on Enable, then close the notebook and maximize the Reversi window on your screen. Now when you press the Print Screen key, a screen image will be sent to your printer.

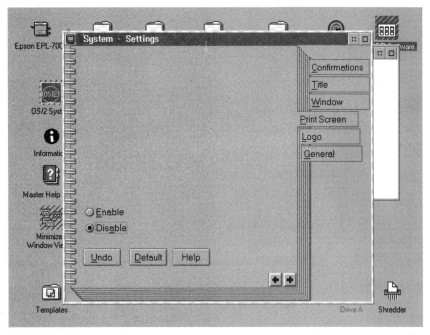

Figure 6-7: The Print Screen page in System Settings notebook.

Disable Print Screen if you are using a third-party utility such as PrntScrn. OS/2's inherent screen print capability is useful for simple tasks, but many times you need more sophistication in formatting the captured image. For that you need a third-party utility such as Mitnor's PrntScrn (used throughout this book). If you do install such a utility, disable OS/2's native Print Screen function to avoid conflicts.

SOLVING THE FONT MYSTERY

Fonts can be one of OS/2's most confusing areas. If you don't care to be absolutely precise about the appearance of your printed and on-screen documents, you can ignore them completely and just use OS/2's default fonts. If you require more control over fonts, you risk stepping into a quagmire of inconsistent and sometimes even contradictory information.

Fonts are something that most people don't think about much, although every day we are confronted with a variety of printed material. Every bit of that printed material is expressed in some font. A font is characterized by a set of attributes called the *font metric,* which includes spacing, pitch, height, style, stroke weight, symbol set and typeface. Often a font is carefully chosen to enhance the impact of the message. If you want to increase the effectiveness of your written communication, controlling fonts is a good place to start.

Screen Fonts vs. Printer Fonts

There are two places on a computer system where fonts are relevant: on the screen and at the printer. The technology for putting characters on the screen is fundamentally different from the technology of putting printed characters on a piece of paper. It is not surprising, therefore, that there are two kinds of fonts, one optimized for display on a screen and the other for placement on paper by a printer.

Nowadays, word processors and other document-generating applications pride themselves on being WYSIWYG (what you see is what you get). However, since your screen font may be only an approximate match for your printer font, what you see on the screen may not be what you get at the printer. OS/2 matches the two kinds of fonts based on their font metrics.

Soft Fonts vs. Hard Fonts

There are two kinds of printer fonts: soft and hard. Soft fonts, also called downloadable fonts, reside on the computer's hard disk. When you want to print a document using one of these fonts, images of each character in the font are sent to the printer along with the document. These images are then used as models for the letters and numbers that appear on paper.

Hard fonts already reside in the printer. They are located on an internal circuit board or on a cartridge plugged into the printer.

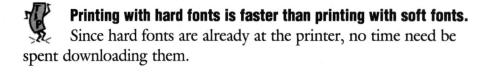 **Printing with hard fonts is faster than printing with soft fonts.** Since hard fonts are already at the printer, no time need be spent downloading them.

Notwithstanding the speed advantage of hard fonts, the trend today is to use soft fonts. If you have a single source for both screen fonts and printer fonts (as when using soft fonts), your chances of getting printed output that looks the same as what you see on the screen are substantially better.

Bitmap Fonts vs. Outline Fonts

Of all the types of soft fonts, bitmap fonts take up the least amount of disk space and are sent to the printer the fastest. They are also the least flexible and produce the crudest images, both on screen and on paper. Different font sizes must be created by resizing a base font.

 If you don't care whether printed output looks exactly like what is on the screen, a bitmap font is ideal. OS/2's standard outline fonts take up more than a megabyte of disk space. You may not want to waste valuable hard disk space on unused fonts. There is also no point in wasting valuable time when OS/2 boots, loading those unused fonts from disk into memory.

Outline fonts, unlike bitmap fonts, do not store images of each character. Instead, a table of characteristics and a formula for putting them together is stored. With this method you can produce a font in any point size (even a fractional point size such as 10.5) with any attribute or combination of attributes. Outline fonts are very flexible, but since they must be computed before they are downloaded, they take longer to prepare for action than bitmap fonts.

 If you want to have the most control of your printouts or screen displays, use outline fonts.

Two types of outline fonts come with OS/2: Adobe Type Manager (ATM) and TrueType. You can get others as well from third-party vendors. These two font families have a major advantage over other fonts in that the screen font is identical (within the limits of the video subsystem) to the printer font of the same name. When you install

OS/2, ATM fonts are installed to work under the WPS, and TrueType
fonts (along with others) are installed to work under WIN-OS/2.
You may optionally add ATM fonts to WIN-OS/2. You may also add
additional fonts of your choice to both environments.

 **Both ATM and TrueType fonts will give you very sharp, well-
formed characters in a wide assortment of sizes.** You may
want to use some of one family and some of the other.

 **If you are pressed for disk space, remove any fonts that you
know you will not need.** A collection of fonts can take up a
significant chunk of real estate on your hard disk.

The Font Palette

The font palette in the System Setup folder is a handy tool for manipulating screen fonts. If you think of all the possible combinations
of point size, typeface, style and emphasis, even a small number of
fonts produces a bewildering array. Most people are only going to
use a few of these. The font palette (Figure 6-8) has room for your
eight favorite screen fonts. Whenever you want to add a new font to
the font palette, you can replace any of the existing ones with whatever new font you specify.

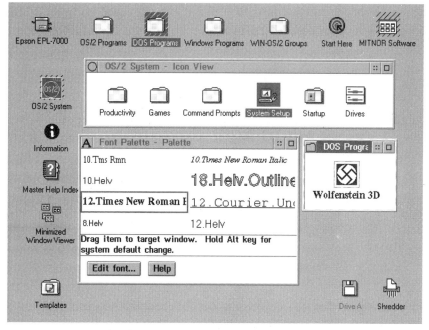

Figure 6-8: The Font Palette showing the DOS Programs window changed to 12-point Times New Roman Bold.

You can change the font of the object names in any folder on the desktop. Do this by dragging a font off the palette and dropping it onto the folder window. Immediately all object names in the folder will be redrawn in the new font.

PRINTING PROBLEMS

Many things must be just right for you to get the printout that you want. If any one of them is wrong, you may get nothing, often with no hint of what is causing the problem. Some things are easy to fix, others not so easy. Listed below are a few common printing problems.

1. The printer is not turned on or is not in the "Ready" state. If this is the problem, after about 45 seconds of trying, OS/2 will tell you that the printer is not connected or ready. After you turn the printer on and the "Online" light is lit, resend the print job.

2. Your printer is turned on and the online light is lit, but OS/2 still tells you the printer is not connected or ready. If there is a printer switch between the computer and the printer, make sure it is set to the right option. If it is not, the system will think (rightly) that the printer is not connected.

3. Your printer is online and the printer switch is in the right position, but the printer still does not receive any signals from the computer. Check the cable. A printer cable contains a couple dozen wires, any one of which could break from too much flexing. Faulty cables are a common source of problems.

4. All the system components discussed above have been verified to be functional, but still there is no printout. Possibly the printer driver software you have is faulty or not properly matched with your printer hardware. Check with the printer manufacturer or on CompuServe and get the latest OS/2 driver for your printer. DOS printer drivers will not work.

5. If the printer still doesn't work, there may be an interrupt conflict. Every peripheral device that is connected to OS/2 communicates through an interrupt request (IRQ) line. If another device has been set to the same IRQ number as your printer, the conflict could cause the printer not to work.

MOVING ON

In this chapter we discussed some of the lesser known things to do before you try to print. We also covered the various ways of performing the print operation itself. The value and tradeoffs of using the spooler were revealed, as was the truth about fonts. Finally some of the most common problems encountered when people try to print something are enumerated, along with possible solutions. In the next chapter we will take a close look at the small demonstration applications (applets) included with OS/2. Some of these are actually useful.

Chapter 7
PRODUCTIVITY PROGRAMS

O S/2 is obviously a great buy. You get the power of a 32-bit multitasking operating system, the reliability of an established product and IBM's legendary support, all for a very attractive price. But that's not all! Included with your purchase of OS/2 you will also receive a complete set of razor sharp Ginsu steak knives! A 35-piece set of stainless steel cookware! Not one, but two bamboo steamers! And a Productivity folder chock full of mini-applications (applets)—all absolutely FREE!

Just kidding! There are no knives, pots or steamers included with OS/2, but the Productivity folder does contain 23 applets (Figure 7-1). Some of them are actually quite useful. Others may be somewhat useful to some people. A few are still waiting patiently for their purpose in life to be revealed.

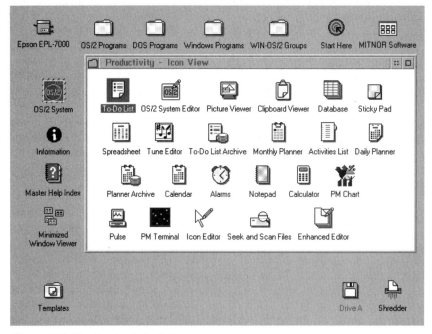

Figure 7-1: The Productivity folder.

MISCELLANEOUS USEFUL APPLETS

The list of applets that I find most useful may not match your list. Oh, well. The functions performed by these programs are so diverse, it's like comparing applets to orangets. Here are my favorites.

System Editor (E.EXE)

In my opinion, the System Editor is OS/2's most useful applet. It doesn't get my vote because it is laden with useful features. In fact it has hardly any, which is why I like it. When I am looking at or editing a text file, I rarely want more than the rudimentary cut, copy and paste functions that are the System Editor's main features. I may want to search for a specific text string in a file. The Find option of the Edit menu provides this capability. Although you can specify font, foreground and background colors and word wrap, if you don't pull down the Options menu, you don't have to be concerned with those little-used features.

If you want to view a text file that does not have any carriage returns until the end of each paragraph, set word wrap on. The text will wrap so that it is all displayed in the window without inserting carriage return codes into the file.

 You can't print a text file directly from the System Editor.

 There are ways to print System Editor files. One way is to save the file, exit the editor and drop the text file's icon onto your printer object. You could also go to command mode and issue a PRINT command or load the file into the Enhanced Editor or a *real* word processor and print it from there.

Enhanced Editor (EPM.EXE)

If the clean, uncluttered, but admittedly Spartan beauty of the System Editor does not appeal to you, the Enhanced Editor offers a number of additional features. You can print from it, specifying printer fonts and styles. You can search for specific text and place bookmarks into the file. This list just scratches the surface of the Enhanced Editor's many features. Online help explains how to use each one.

 The Enhanced Editor puts a carriage return–line feed character into the text you are entering whenever you hit the right margin. If you are entering commands into a command file, this behavior may have the undesirable effect of chopping a command in two.

 Use the System Editor for command files and the Enhanced Editor for plain text files.

Icon Editor

Every object on the OS/2 desktop has an icon associated with it. Some of these icons are quite evocative and remind us immediately of the object that they represent. Unfortunately, others are not very helpful at all, such as the one shown in Figure 7-2.

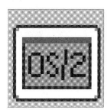

Figure 7-2: A not very meaningful icon.

Figure 7-2 shows the default icon that OS/2 assigns to any program if another icon is not provided. It is neither informative nor inspiring. You can use the icon editor to either transfer an existing icon from an icon library to the application or to draw a new icon from scratch. Either way, the result is bound to be an improvement over the default.

Let us say that you have written a simulation of the view out of the forward window of a starship that is capable of approaching the speed of light. As the ship reaches relativistic velocities, Doppler shifting of starlight becomes evident until a starbow forms. It would be nice if the icon for your program reminded the user of stars. Follow these steps to give your program a new icon:

1. Search your icon library, if you have one, for an icon you consider appropriate.

2. Open the Icon Editor in the Productivity folder. If you have found a suitable icon, select Open from the Icon Editor's File menu and specify the drive, directory and name of the icon file in the dialog box that appears.

3. If you want to build your own icon, start with the empty workspace shown in Figure 7-3. The workspace is a magnified image of the 32x32 bitmap that is used to construct icons. At the upper left is an actual size replica of the workspace that will show you, as you build it, what the icon will look like.

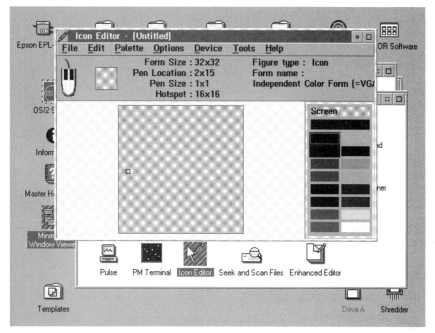

Figure 7-3: The Icon Editor workspace.

4. Select Grid from the Options menu to overlay a **32x32** grid on the workspace. This will help you proportion your drawing.

5. Draw your icon. Use colors from the palette on the right and other tools from the menu at the top.

6. When you are satisfied with the new icon, save it to an .ICO file. The new file name will appear in the title bar of the Icon Editor window (Figure 7-4).

7. Close the Icon Editor and open the Settings notebook of your application.

8. Click on the General tab to show the page dealing with icons (Figure 7-5).

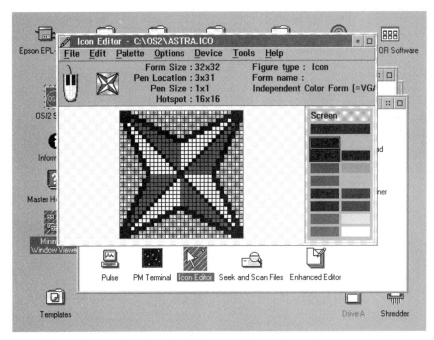

Figure 7-4: The new icon has been drawn and saved.

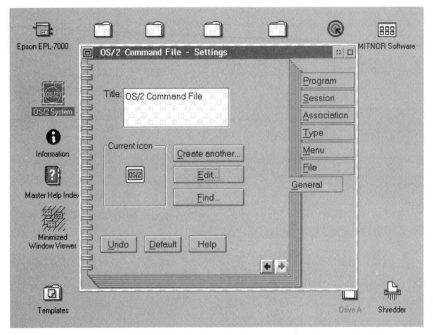

Figure 7-5: The Settings notebook Icon page.

9. Click on the Find button to find the .ICO file that you have created (or that you selected from an icon library).

10. In the Find dialog box, enter the folder that contains the icon (if you know it) and the name of the icon.

11. If you are not certain of the location of the icon, click on Search all subfolders before clicking on Find. A Find Results dialog box should appear with your icon in it (Figure 7-6).

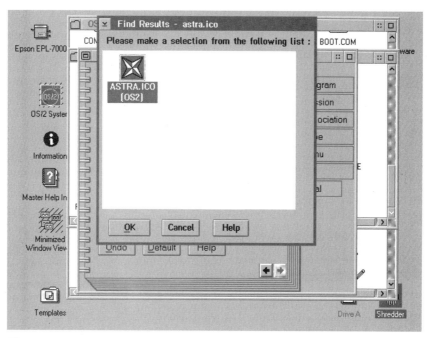

Figure 7-6: The new icon has been found.

12. Select OK to trigger the icon change. Your program is now represented by the new icon, as shown in Figure 7-7.

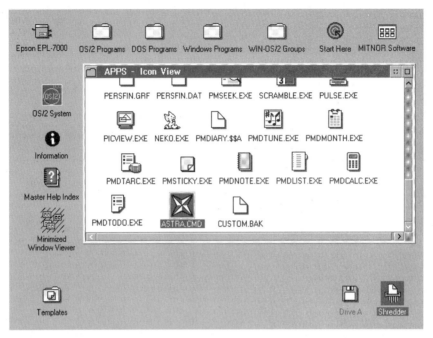

Figure 7-7: The ASTRA.CMD program is now represented by the new icon.

 It is not necessary to invoke the Icon Editor from the Productivity folder. It can be called directly from the General page of your program's Settings notebook by clicking on the Edit button. When you create an icon this way it is incorporated directly into the application and does not have an independent existence as an .ICO file. Using the Icon Editor results in two images of the icon: one in a file with an .ICO extension and the other incorporated into its underlying application.

You may want to retain the .ICO file as a possible starting point for a related icon that you may want to design later.

Seek and Scan Files

While the System Editor is the applet that I find most useful, Seek and Scan Files ranks as a close second. It seems that I lose track of more files nowadays than I did a few years ago. This is probably because I have more files to lose. Also, the Workplace Shell paradigm encourages me to create folders and move files around among them. It is easy to forget where an object is.

Happily, I can afford to be forgetful as long as I have Seek and Scan Files. It will find a file anywhere on the system as long as I remember the file's name. It will even find a file if I don't remember its name, as long as I remember some character string contained in the file.

Although Seek and Scan Files can find any file by its filename, or any file containing text by a text string, it is optimized for finding command files. CONFIG.SYS, AUTOEXEC.BAT and STARTUP.CMD are all examples of command files. By convention, any file with an extension of .BAT or .CMD is a command file. Such files are ASCII text files that are directly executed by either the OS/2 or DOS command processor.

Figure 7-8 shows the Seek and Scan Files dialog box after the completion of a search of drive C for all files with a file name starting with ASTRA.

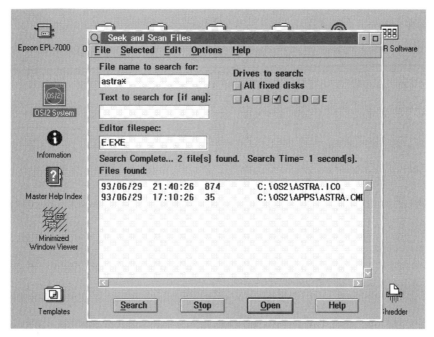

Figure 7-8: The Seek and Scan Files dialog box.

OS/2 syntax is different from DOS's when handling wildcard characters. It resembles UNIX syntax more than DOS syntax in this area. For this same retrieval DOS would require "astra*.*"; OS/2 allows that but also accepts "astra*."

Figure 7-8 shows an interesting thing. The file ASTRA.CMD takes up only 35 bytes, but the icon file ASTRA.ICO that we associated with it using the ASTRA.CMD Settings notebook is 874 bytes. How can that be? When an icon is associated with a file, it is included into that file. How can an 874 byte icon be *included* into a 35 byte command file?

The answer is that the icon is included not in the file, but rather in the extended attributes of that file. In this case, the file's extended attributes are far larger than the file itself.

Another thing to notice in Figure 7-8 is the field labeled "Editor filespec:." The default entry here is E.EXE, which is the file name of the System Editor.

You can replace the default entry with the filename of the editor of your choice. For example, to invoke the Enhanced Editor, replace E.EXE with EPM.EXE. Once you have made such a change, the new editor will remain as the default.

If you were to select a text file from the Seek and Scan list of files found, then click on the Open button, the designated editor would open the file. You could then edit the file without leaving the Seek and Scan Files applet.

This is where it becomes clear that Seek and Scan Files is optimized for use with command files. After you have modified the command file, you can run it immediately to see if it works as expected. Again, this happens without leaving the Seek and Scan Files application. With the command file once again selected in the Files found: list, pull down the Selected menu and click on Process. The command file will be run, then control will be returned to Seek and Scan Files. In this way you may go through several iterations of command file development and execution without ever switching contexts. It is very convenient.

Besides Process, there are two other options on the Selected menu: Open and Command. The Open option duplicates the Open button at the bottom of the Seek and Scan Files dialog box. Use whichever one you find most convenient. The Command option allows you to execute an operating system command directly, once again without leaving Seek and Scan Files.

The Options menu offers several choices you can make about the way a search is conducted. You can choose to search only the current directory, with or without subdirectories. You can choose to display each instance of the search text that is found, in addition to the specifications of the file that holds it. You can choose to ignore case in the search, or to find only instances where the case in the file is the same as the case in the search string. You can also choose to clear the Files found: list before a new search is instituted, or to leave previously found files displayed.

Clipboard Viewer

The OS/2 Clipboard is pretty simple. It holds an image of a snapshot of the screen. The image may be either a graphical bitmap image or a text image. Clipboard can tell the difference and display each appropriately. With the WIN-OS/2 clipboard set to the public state, which is the default, graphical images or text data saved on the WIN-OS/2 clipboard are instantly available on the OS/2 clipboard also.

If your WIN-OS/2 clipboard is set to public, an image saved to it will also replace anything that had been saved on your OS/2 clipboard.

PERSONAL INFORMATION MANAGER

One of the best ways to improve your productivity is to organize the tasks that need to be done, prioritize them and plan for their timely execution. Many paper-based systems have been developed over the years to help people be more efficient. These systems have been helpful but have limited usefulness because they lack intelligence and require considerable work on the part of the person using them.

The idea of putting these functions on a small computer has gained considerable popularity recently. The software written has acquired the name personal information manager (PIM). A number of the applets included with OS/2 have been designed to work together to form a personal information manager. If you put OS/2 on a notebook computer, you can carry your PIM with you wherever you go and refer to it frequently. The OS/2 PIM may be valuable to you even on a desktop computer if you spend much of your time at your desk.

Daily Planner

The Daily Planner is the core application of the personal information manager. It creates the master planning file that the other applets use. When you open it, a blank page of your new computerized daily planner is displayed (Figure 7-9).

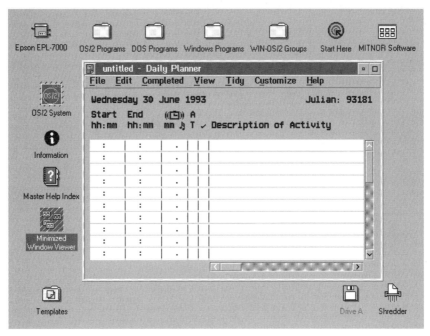

Figure 7-9: A new Daily Planner page.

Spaces for ten activities (available with VGA video) are shown. If you maximize the Daily Planner window, you can view eighteen activities with more room for descriptions. These are not rigid limits, since the vertical scroll bar allows you to schedule as many activities as any reasonable person would want. The horizontal scroll bar accommodates descriptions of up to 180 characters.

Each row on the Daily Planner form has start and end times for the activity and an alarm field (signified by the graphic of a ringing alarm clock). If you wish, you can set the alarm to sound a designated number of minutes before the scheduled start of an activity. This gives you advance warning of appointments and is also useful in keeping you from spending too much time on a single activity.

Let's put some sample data into the Daily Planner to see how it works. Figure 7-10 shows the current page after one activity has been entered. The first scheduled activity is a Toastmasters meeting at 6:30 in the morning. The Description of Activity field is short in this case but may be up to 180 characters. You may also select one of 32 icons, which takes up two character positions in the description.

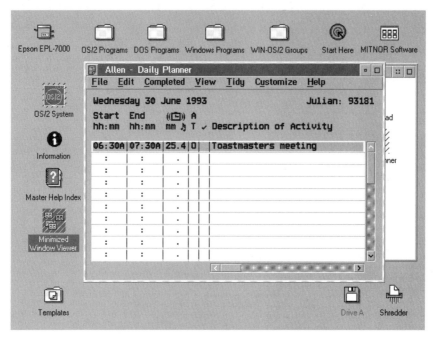

Figure 7-10: A first Entry has been made in Daily Planner.

Get your AMs and PMs correct. Manually enter the A or P after specifying start and end times. If you do not, Planner will make an assumption and choose for you. If your first activity starts at 8:00 or later, Planner assumes it is a morning activity. If your first activity starts at 7:59 or earlier, it assumes your first activity is an afternoon or evening activity. In the case of the Toastmasters meeting above, it was necessary to manually enter 6:30A and 7:30A.

In some ways, this applet is not so intelligent. If you enter a start of 6:30A and an end of 7:30, it will assume the end time is 7:30 PM. A thirteen hour activity! I guess we can't complain too much, considering the price.

The 25.4 in the alarm column means that I want to be warned **25** minutes before the start of the meeting by the playing of tune #4, "La Cucaracha," which is just the kind of up-tempo song I need to get me out the door in the morning. The O in the Activity Type (AT) column shows that this is an Out-of-office activity. Set this attribute from the Activity Type submenu of the Edit menu (Figure 7-11).

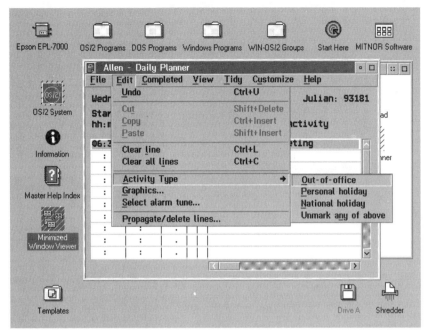

Figure 7-11: Activity Type submenu.

Any activity that does not have an entry in the AT column is assumed to be a normal office activity. Choices on the submenu are Out-of-office, Personal holiday and National holiday. Figure 7-11 also shows how to choose a new alarm tune. You need not listen to "La Cucaracha" for every event. When you choose the Select alarm tune... option from the Edit menu, you can choose from several dozen songs. You can use a different tune for each activity if you wish.

Alarms

Before an alarm will go off, you must independently activate the Alarms applet and link it to the master file you have created with the Daily Planner. From the Alarms Customize menu select Set master planner file. Next select the desired file from the list (Figure 7-12).

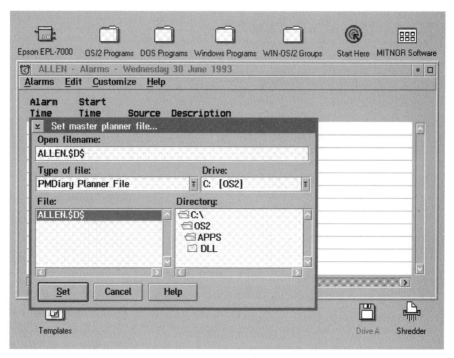

Figure 7-12: Select a master planner file.

In our case there is only one file to choose from because we have just started. If several people are using the same system, they could each have their own master planner file, identifying it with their names. My file is ALLEN.D. Press the Set button to establish the link to the master planner file.

Now the appointment is shown in the Alarms window (Figure 7-13). At 6:05 AM on Wednesday morning, my computer will break out with the opening few measures of "La Cucaracha." I will instantly associate this with Toastmasters and head out for the meeting.

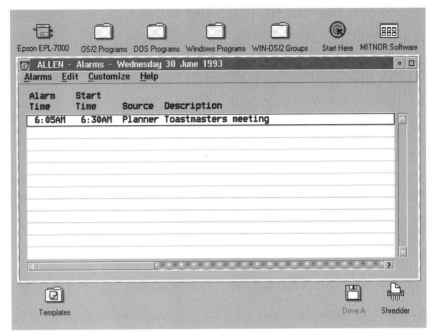

Figure 7-13: The Alarms list with Toastmaster entry from Daily Planner.

 If you have a meeting that occurs regularly, you can enter all occurrences, complete with alarm, with a single procedure.

One of the options on the Edit menu shown in Figure 7-11 is Propagate/delete lines. When you select it, the dialog box shown in Figure 7-14 pops up.

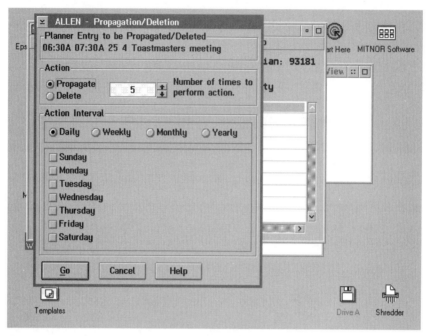

Figure 7-14: The Propagation/Deletion dialog box.

The event to propagate is shown at the top (Toastmasters meeting). You can specify the number of times to propagate it into the future and decide whether to list it daily, weekly, monthly or yearly. In this case, we want to schedule this event weekly for the next year. The maximum number of times the action will propagate is 50, which is close enough to a year for our purposes. Make sure the Propagate radio button is selected and the Action Interval is set to Weekly. Specify Every Week for the interval (Figure 7-15).

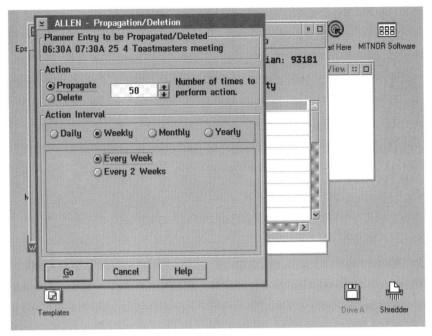

Figure 7-15: Propagation for the coming year's Toastmasters meetings.

Press the Go button when everything is right. You have just scheduled a year's worth of Toastmasters meetings. If your computer is on and the Alarms applet is active at 6:05 next Wednesday morning, it will play a tune to remind you to go to your meeting.

Tune Editor

Maybe "La Cucaracha" is not your favorite song. Some people do not appreciate Latin music. Others just do not like songs about bugs. You are not stuck with the 37 songs provided with OS/2, all of which are so old that their copyrights have run out. You can use the Tune Editor to key in one of your contemporary favorites, one of your own compositions or a song that has special meaning for the occasion. For example, you could give yourself up to 59 minutes warning of your upcoming wedding by playing "Here Comes the Bride" as the appointed hour approached.

You can use either the mouse or the keyboard to enter the song of your choice (Figure 7-16). Once you have entered a song, save it to a new or an already existing tune file. The original alarm tune file is named PMDIARY.$$A. Any tune files you create will also have a $$A extension.

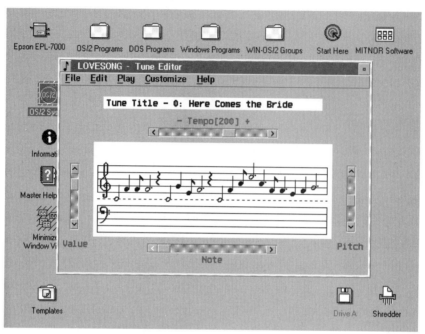

Figure 7-16: A newly entered song.

The Alarms applet will not automatically play your newly created tunes. After you spend a lot of time and bother numerous family members or colleagues by playing progressively less imperfect renditions of your songs, you will find that the Alarms applet will only play the tunes in the PMDIARY.$$A file.

To substitute your tunes for the defaults, rename PMDIARY.$$A. Use a name like OLDSONGS.$$A. Next rename your tune file to PMDIARY.$$A. Alarms will now use your tune file.

Daily Planner Reprise

Once you have completed one or more of your planned activities, you get to enjoy the sense of accomplishment that comes from telling your Daily Planner that you have done so. There are several ways to do this. You can use the Completed menu (Figure 7-17).

The first group of options have to do with the currently selected line only. The second group perform the same operations but on all entries on the current page.

If you select "Mark line as completed," Planner will put a check-mark in the completed column for the current line. A record of your completion of the item will remain on the Planner page for that day.

The "Mark line and add to archive" option is similar, but in addition to marking the completed column, Planner will also transfer this entry to the Daily Planner Archive file. This provides a more permanent record of your activities.

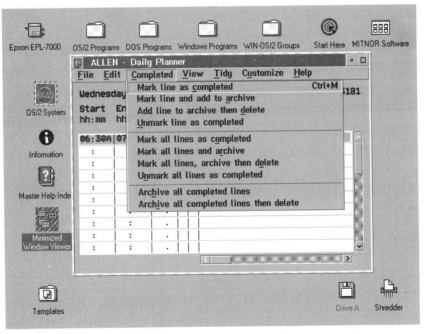

Figure 7-17: The Completed menu of the Daily Planner.

 You may choose to archive your more significant accomplishments, while only placing a checkmark by the others.

"Add line to archive then delete" is for people who like to keep their Planner clean and uncluttered. After archiving a completed activity, it is erased from the Daily Planner. With this method you can concentrate fully on those tasks that are yet to be done.

Finally, "Unmark line as completed" comes in handy when you think you have completed as task, but it later becomes evident that you have not. For example, a task might be "Develop new wholesale price sheet." You do so and check it off. Five minutes later one of your salespeople comes in to inform you that a major competitor has just lowered prices and is getting all the business. It is time to un-mark the line and start working on the price list again.

What you can do for the current line, you can also do for all the lines on the current page. You also have the option of selectively archiving all completed lines on the page or archiving all of them and then deleting them. Planner gives you a lot of options so you can work in the way that you find most comfortable and still provide the system with the data it needs to keep accurate records.

The archive file you create, then periodically update from the Daily Planner Completed menu, is accessible for inspection by choosing the Planner Archive icon from the Productivity folder. Whenever you want to review your accomplishments, click on its icon and select the desired archive file. In my case, that file is ALLEN.$DA. This can give you a real psychological boost on a day when you are depressed and feel like you are not getting very much done.

Monthly Planner

The Monthly Planner uses the same master planning file as the Daily Planner, giving you an overview of your activities over the span of a month. A two-character space is allotted to every hour of every day, giving a breakdown of activities to the nearest half hour.

Every event recorded in the master planning file with the Daily Planner is represented in the monthly planner. The first two characters of the Description of Activity field represent the activity. If you selected one of the two-character graphical icons as the first two characters of the description field, the icon will be displayed in the appropriate time slot for that activity. If you entered text, as we did for the Toastmasters meeting, then the first two characters of text will be displayed.

Whenever you mark a task as completed on the Daily Planner, the color of the icon will change on the Monthly Planner.

 If you are looking at the current month, a cursor will be flashing at the current time on the current day. This will immediately tell you whether you are on schedule or not. If uncompleted tasks are still present to the left of the cursor, you are behind.

If you get tense from being scheduled to the nearest half hour, mellow out. You control what activities you schedule, and you determine what constitutes "completion." Set the system up and run it so it helps you to get more done, but not in such a way that you start getting ulcers.

Activities List

The Activities List provides yet another way to view the information in your master planning file. The format is the same as that for the Daily Planner Archive. All the activities in your file are listed, from today until your last planned activity. If you have planned out 50 weeks, you will see 50 weeks of entries. If you have planned an annual activity out 50 years, you will see that.

Calendar

The Calendar applet is also connected to the master planning file. It provides a compact view of a month's activities. Figure 7-18 shows an example. Weekdays are shown in a different color than weekend days. Days that have one or more scheduled activities are enclosed in boxes. Days with an out-of-office activity are shown in a different color. Today is also differentiated from the other days by color. If you double-click on any day, the daily planner page for that day pops up. You can make changes or additions. Click on the minimize widget in the upper right corner of the Daily Planner window to return to the calendar. You can view any month of any year. If your master planning file contains activities for the month, they will be indicated. If no activities exist yet, you can use the Daily Planner to enter them.

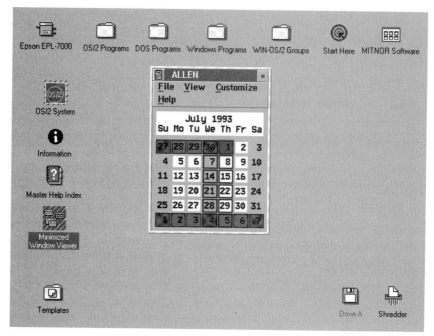

Figure 7-18: A Calendar month.

To-Do List

The To-Do List is a prioritized list of tasks that you want to complete. It is not connected to the master planner file.

The To-Do List may be enough. If you want to organize your day and address the most important tasks first but without maintaining a full-blown PIM, the To-Do List may be just the tool for you. It is simple and easy to use. Frankly, it is not much different from keeping a To-Do List on paper. Figure 7-19 shows a sample To-Do List. Entries are sorted first by priority, then by date. Completed tasks are marked as Done and are shown in a different color.

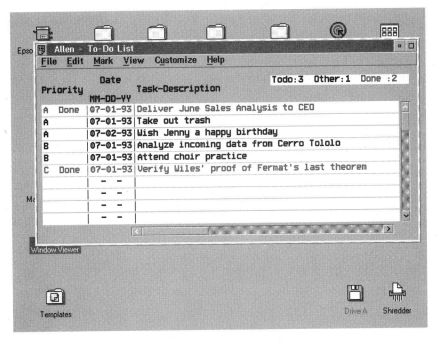

Figure 7-19: A sample To-Do List.

To-Do List Archive

The To-Do List Archive works the same way the Daily Planner Archive works. From the To-Do List menu you can archive completed tasks to form a permanent record. These entries are sent to the To-Do List Archive, which you can view from this applet.

Notepad

The Notepad works like a small deck of electronic index cards. You can write things on each one and flip from one to another with the mouse or a menu selection. You can save different notepads under different names. My question is, "Do I need a computer for this?" I don't think so. I am reminded of one of the original justifications for having a home computer: "You can keep your recipes on it." Emulating a 25-cent deck of cards is hardly justification for buying a $1,000 computer. I suppose you might find a use for it.

If you have any important data, don't keep it in the Notepad.
Buy a real database management system and keep it there.
That way you will be sure that you are able to retrieve the information you want when you want it.

Sticky Pad

The Sticky Pad is an electronic replica of a pad of 3M Post-it© notes.
You can attach these notes to windows on your desktop. Figure 7-20
shows such a note attached to a To-Do List window.

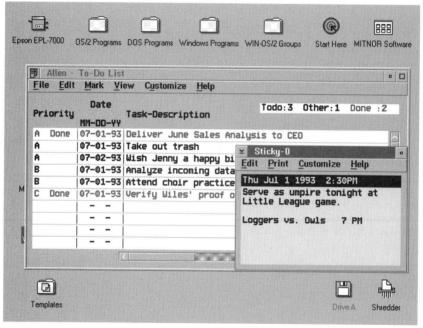

Figure 7-20: A Sticky Pad note.

Don't bother with the Sticky Pad. Buy the real thing and stick
them to your video monitor frame. They are inexpensive, easy
to use and do not obscure any of the text on the screen unless you
want them to.

STRIPPED DOWN MINI-APPLICATIONS

Whereas some of the applets included with OS/2—such as the editors and the Seek and Scan Files program—have modest ambitions and do a good job of living up to them, others pretend to be something they are not, and thus are almost sure to disappoint.

The applets that remain to be mentioned are essentially stripped-down versions of applications that are available commercially. In general, if the work you are doing is even moderately serious or important to you, you should use a commercial application. The money you spend on the purchase price will be more than repaid by the extra hours you do *not* spend trying to do the job with an inadequate tool.

Database

The Database applet is actually a file manager, with limited capability. You can use it as the basis for a telephone dialer, however, by storing telephone numbers in it and using it in conjunction with your modem. The procedure for setting this up is rather complex and can more easily be done with a good commercial telecommunications package. If you have a modem, you probably already have such a program anyway.

 If you need to store anything more complex than recipes, get a real DBMS rather than relying on the Database applet.

Spreadsheet

The Spreadsheet applet would be a disappointment to a user of the original VisiCalc, let alone people familiar with recent releases of Lotus 1-2-3, Borland Quattro Pro or Microsoft Excel.

 If you do any kind of numerical manipulations, get a real spreadsheet rather than trying to use the Spreadsheet applet.

PM Chart

PM Chart comes a lot closer to being a real application than do the other disappointing items mentioned in this section. It incorporates a rudimentary spreadsheet and graphics tools you can use to convert spreadsheet numbers into charts and graphs. It was written by Micro-grafx, Inc., and is a limited version of a product they sell commercial-ly. The "fit and finish" of this program is definitely a cut above the other applets provided with OS/2. Still, important capabilities have been left out.

 If you are going to be charting numeric data kept in spreadsheets, buy the full-blown product from Micrografx.

PM Terminal

PM Terminal is a terminal emulator and communications package lacking most of the features you would find in a commercial product.

 If you spend much time on line, don't try to use PM Terminal. Just about any commercial or shareware program is better.

Picture Viewer

The Picture Viewer is for viewing metafiles (.MET), picture inter-change format files (.PIF), and spooler files (.SPL). I don't have much occasion to look at any of these kinds of files. If you do, you may find Picture Viewer useful.

When Picture Viewer is running, it can use large amounts of memory. If you are already using your SWAPPER file pretty heavily, Picture Viewer could push it over the edge.

Pulse

Pulse gives you a real-time visual display of how heavily your system resources are being used from moment to moment. Figure 7-21 shows a maximized Pulse window as it appears during a Seek and Scan Files operation. The display is not calibrated, and it essentially tells you when your hard disk is accessing and when it is not. I can deduce this information by listening to the clicks coming from inside my computer.

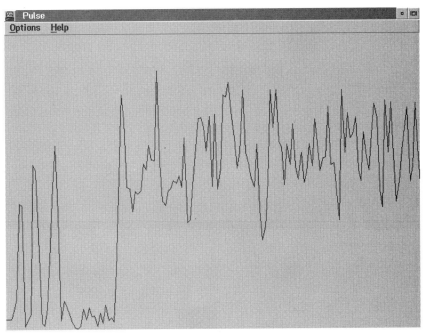

Figure 7-21: The Pulse window.

Pulse may be of some value to advanced users in optimizing their systems' settings. You can look at Pulse while performing an operation, perhaps triggering Print Screen to record how hard the CPU has worked on the task just completed. Then you can change a parameter such as PRIORITY or THREADS and run the same operation again. Pulse will tell you if the CPU is having a harder or an easier time with the new settings.

Calculator

The Calculator applet is an emulation of a standard electronic calculator that would cost you close to three dollars if you had to buy it. Calculator would be a handy thing to have on the desktop if it weren't for one small fact. The calculator that comes with WIN-OS/2 is much better. The standard version of the WIN-OS/2 calculator does everything the OS/2 version does plus more. It is also somewhat easier to use, with larger keys. The greatest benefit of the WIN-OS/2 calculator, however, is that you can switch to Scientific mode, converting it into a full function scientific calculator that works in hexadecimal, octal and binary, as well as conventional decimal.

Use the WIN-OS/2 Calculator rather than the one in the Productivity folder. There is no point in having two calculators on your desktop, and the WIN-OS/2 one is much more capable. Just make sure you migrate it when you install OS/2.

MOVING ON

When I was young, my mother sometimes came home from the grocery store with something called a Kellogg's Variety Pack. It contained eight small boxes of various kinds of cereal. Some my brothers and I liked, others stayed on the shelf.

The applets included with OS/2 are similar. You will probably find some of them indispensable and use them every day. Others will remain on the shelf. You might find a use for them some day. If you get in the habit of using your personal information manager, the gain in personal efficiency could be worth a great deal to you.

OS/2 is the first popular 32-bit multitasking operating system for Intel-based personal computers. Microsoft's Windows NT is now available, too. Many people would like to perform direct comparisons of the two systems. The most accurate comparison results from installing both operating systems on the same hardware. The next chapter tells you how to install and run OS/2 2.1 and Windows NT 3.1 on the same machine at the same time.

Chapter 8

INSTALLATION MAGIC

So far in this book, we have assumed that you are using an OS/2 system that someone else has already installed. If so, you are lucky because you are spared the work of setting it up yourself. On the other hand, you may be unlucky because the initial installation is perhaps not exactly what you would have chosen for yourself.

At any rate, sooner or later you may find yourself installing (or reinstalling) OS/2. If you do, a little extra knowledge can save you hours or even days of frustration. If you do not have all the required ingredients or do not combine them in the proper way, OS/2 will not install.

THE SIZE OF OS/2

One of the first surprises about OS/2 to a DOS user is how *big* it is. DOS can be run from a 360k floppy disk in a system with 640k or less of RAM and no hard disk storage. To go from a character-based, single-tasking operating system to a multitasking operating system with a graphical user interface is a big step in capability. It brings with it a big step in resource requirements.

Disk Space Requirements

IBM recommends that a system have at least 50mb of hard disk space available to install OS/2. If you have one or more sizable applications, you will undoubtedly need more. A complete installation of OS/2 uses about 35mb, not counting the space that will be used by the Swapper (explained below).

As you load more applications into OS/2, it dynamically adjusts by using more memory. When it runs out of memory, it starts using disk space, too. When it runs out of disk space, files may be damaged. You may have to reload the operating system from scratch.

Back up frequently. You can always reload OS/2 from the installation disks. All you will lose is the time you spend rebuilding the system. Your data files, however, may be irreplaceable.

Partial Installations

One way to save more disk space for applications and data is to install only those parts of OS/2 that you will need. You may not need to install everything. After you have selected the items that you want to install, OS/2 will tell you how much disk space it will take and how much you have available.

If you have limited disk space, you can subtract and then re-add system features until you have the most important capabilities and are still within your memory budget.

After you install your peripheral devices, through a screen that looks similar to Figure 8-1, another screen is displayed (Figure 8-2) listing optional features to install. Place a checkmark in the box to the left of each feature you want to install. Beside each option in the window is an indication of the number of bytes it requires. The first six choices on the Setup and Installation screen have a More button to the right. These choices can be broken down into parts. You may choose to install some parts but not others.

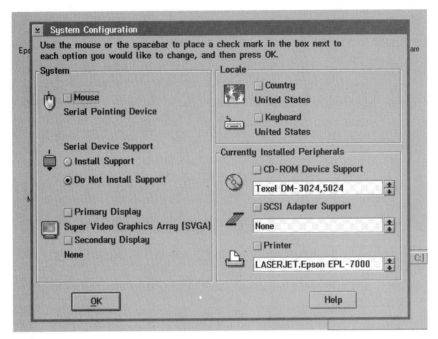

Figure 8-1: The System Configuration screen.

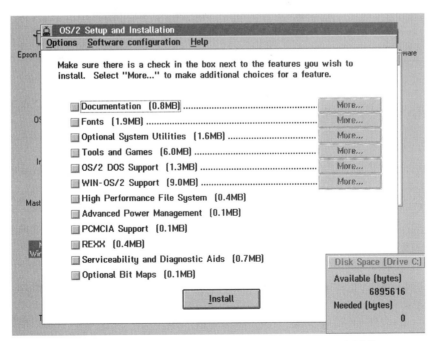

Figure 8-2: Setup and Installation screen for optional features of OS/2.

The largest memory consumer on the list is WIN-OS/2 Support. If you know that you will never want to run any Windows applications, you can leave out WIN-OS/2 support and save a cool 9mb. Even if you want to keep WIN-OS/2 support, you may not need all of it. Since WIN-OS/2 Support has a More button, there are optional parts of it that you may choose not to install. Check WIN-OS/2, then click on More (Figure 8-3).

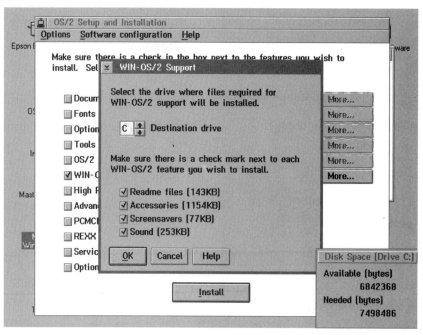

Figure 8-3: The WIN-OS/2 Support window.

The window in the bottom right corner of the screen shows that there is not enough disk space available to install everything that is currently selected. This is not necessarily a disaster. The installation program allows you to place WIN-OS/2 on a different disk. Also, if you are doing a reinstall, you will be copying files over the top of files that are already taking up space on your disk. The only space needed on a reinstall is that required by new files that were not present before.

If you have already read WIN-OS/2's readme files, you may decide not to put them on your hard disk. You may also elect to leave out the accessories, screen savers or sound. Analyze your needs and work patterns carefully. You do not want to eliminate anything that you will later wish you had kept. Of course, if you do mistakenly leave off something useful, you can always install it later using OS/2's Selective Install feature.

After WIN-OS/2, the next largest optional category is Tools and Games. If you leave out the Terminal Emulator you will save 1.6mb. PMChart takes up 1.2mb. Klondike Solitaire, which is very similar to the Solitaire included with WIN-OS/2, takes up almost 400k. OS/2 Chess plays a very weak game and is probably not worth the 266k it takes up.

By selectively leaving out features you are not likely to use, your savings in disk space can be substantial. The more space you save, the more that will be available for your own programs and data files.

System Memory Requirements

If magic has to do with the apparent suspension of the ordinary laws of nature, then the fact that OS/2 has virtual memory is perhaps its most magical feature. A computer system with virtual memory behaves as if it has more memory than is actually installed.

You can load and run programs that are larger than your memory. This sounds pretty amazing, since it seems to violate that ancient proverb, "There ain't no such thing as a free lunch (TANSTAAFL)." It also seems to contradict "What you see is what you get (WYSIWYG)" and the conservation of mass-energy ($E=MC^2$).

Well, relax. Your faith in the physical laws formulated by Newton, Einstein and Heinlein is still well founded. Virtual memory is not really magic. There is a trick to it.

The Swapper

When OS/2 is installed, a file is created on one of your hard disks named SWAPPER.DAT. It starts out as small as 1mb but can grow to take up almost all the available space on its disk. SWAPPER.DAT, the swap file, is the secret behind virtual memory.

Although OS/2 may have multiple programs in memory at the same time, they are not all likely to be active. Some are probably waiting for a keystroke or a mouse click from the user. Those that are loaded but not active do not need to be taking up space in your high speed semiconductor memory (RAM). Thus when you load a new application or do something else that puts fresh demands on the memory, one or more of the quiescent jobs can be swapped out to the swap file on disk. The inactive job is not doing anything anyway, so it might as well be doing nothing on a relatively slow disk rather than in very fast but less capacious RAM. When that job becomes active again, it will be swapped into RAM after another job is swapped out to disk.

Virtual memory is a great concept. It allows you to run large programs or several smaller programs on hardware that otherwise could not run them at all. There really is no such thing as a free lunch, however. The penalty here is reduced access time.

When OS/2 runs out of RAM and starts to swap to disk, operations slow down perceptibly. Since the access times for disk drives are about 100,000 times slower than the access times for RAM (~10 ms vs. ~100 ns), when you start writing large blocks of memory out to disk, overall performance is bound to suffer.

If your system is slowing down frequently due to swapping, install more RAM. The quickest and easiest fix to slowdowns in a computer with a virtual memory system is to add more real memory, so the virtual memory feature doesn't have to kick in until you have placed a substantially greater load on it.

Virtual memory is the feature that allows IBM to claim that OS/2 will run in a system with no more than 4mb of memory. 4mb is really not enough for OS/2, but with virtual memory, it will work.

If you try to run OS/2 on a 4mb system, it will start swapping right away. Almost anything you do will cause the swapper to be called into play. I guarantee you will not be happy with the system's performance.

Do not put OS/2 on any system that has less than 6mb of RAM. With 6mb you should be able to run at least one moderately sized application without resorting to swapping.

Do not install the IBM Multimedia Presentation Manager/2 on a system with less than 8mb.

Install as much RAM as you can afford. The more you have, the better your system will perform, the fewer error messages you will see, and the more windows you can have open on your desktop. 6mb is about 10 times better than 4mb. 8mb is substantially better than 6mb. 16mb is somewhat better than 8mb. Clearly the law of diminishing returns is active here. However, RAM is relatively inexpensive. 16mb is a good amount to have. If you are a real speed freak or do serious multimedia work, you probably want to pop for 32mb.

What Activities Use a Lot of Memory?

Some applications have a greater appetite for memory than others and may cause you to dip into your swap file. High resolution graphics, high fidelity sound, animation and multimedia in general are all big consumers of memory. Spooling print jobs also eats into memory. If you are printing a series of high resolution graphics files, you may not only start swapping, but your swap file will start to grow. You don't have to do any of these things, however, to initiate swapping. Just opening numerous windows and leaving them open will eventually use up all your RAM and cause swapping to start.

Don't leave windows laying around open on your desktop. Open windows consume more memory than closed ones. Close them when you are finished with them unless you plan to get right back to them. You can always open them again.

The Horror of a Swap File Explosion

When the swap file is created at install time, it is given a nominal size—2mb for example. As the swap file starts to be used, it commandeers more disk space as it needs it. As requirements decrease, it shrinks back to its nominal size. If the demand for memory becomes too great, the swap file may grow to fill almost all of available disk space, leaving insufficient room for any data your applications may try to write to disk.

OS/2 warns you when your swap file is approaching the limits of your disk. When this happens, pull back and close as many jobs as you can to free up swapper space. On the other hand, you could decide to follow the advice of Admiral David Farragut who, when told that torpedoes were in the water at the Battle of Mobile Bay, said, "Damn the torpedoes, full speed ahead." You can proceed without changing anything. If you do, you may get away with it, as Farragut did. Alternatively, the swapper may try to expand into an area already filled with programs. This could cause OS/2 to fail, corrupting the data in any files that are open and possibly some that are not. Don't let this happen to you.

FILE SYSTEMS

Computer data is stored in files on magnetic and optical disks. The operating system controls the organization of those files and the method of accessing them. Since OS/2 is backward compatible with DOS, it must be able to read and write DOS files as well as those created strictly for use with OS/2. The DOS FAT file system is different from the OS/2 HPFS structure. You may choose to use either one or both of the formats. There are advantages and disadvantages to each.

FAT

The DOS file system uses a File Allocation Table (FAT) to organize the location of files on a disk. This scheme first saw widespread use when it appeared with DOS 1.0 on the first IBM PC in 1981. That first PC had a theoretical memory limit of 640k and could be equipped with either one or two 160k floppy disk drives. You could order a PC with as little as 16k of RAM, but many early customers opted to really load it up—with 64k.

The FAT system relies on breaking the disk up into units called clusters and writing files to the disk one cluster after another. The File Allocation Table keeps track of what piece of what file is stored in each cluster. As time goes on and obsolete files are erased, the "holes" left by the erased files are filled in with chunks of new files.

This system works well since disk space can be used again and again. Files that you no longer use regularly, but want to keep, can be archived onto tape or floppy. Data that you know you won't need again can be erased. Ideally, you will always have room for your current projects.

Unfortunately, there are a couple of problems with this rosy scenario. One problem is *fragmentation*. The other is the typical user's gradual, but inevitable, need for ever-increasing amounts of disk space.

FRAGMENTATION

When you install your first set of files on a newly formatted disk, each one is written sequentially. Each file is composed of a contiguous set of clusters. Once the read/write mechanism settles on the first byte of the first cluster, it can read (or write) the entire file in one continuous operation. This is the best case; system response is the fastest.

The situation changes, however, after you have erased one or more files. The next file you add will probably not be exactly the same size as the one you erased. The number of clusters left vacant may not be enough for the new file. In that case, DOS puts as much of the file into the first hole as it can, then proceeds to the second hole and puts as much there as it can, and so on until the file is completely written to disk. The file may end up divided into several groups of clusters or *fragments*. Now when you read this file, the read/write mechanism must jump from one cluster to another, or even from one track to another to access the entire thing. These mechanical movement operations require time, resulting in a general slowing down of disk performance. As more and more files "turn over" on the disk, performance progressively gets worse.

If there has been considerable file turnover on your disk and you notice performance degradation, try defragmenting the disk. There are two ways to defragment a disk. One is to use a commercially available defragmenting utility. This is known as in-place defragmenting. The other is to back up all your files to tape or floppy, erase them from your hard disk then restore from your backup medium. There is a certain element of risk associated with either of these defragmenting strategies. If you were to experience a power failure or other interruption in the middle of an in-place defragmentation operation, some or all of your files may be corrupted and unrecoverable. Back up your hard disk before attempting to do an in-place defragmentation.

Do not use a DOS defragmentation utility to defragment an OS/2 disk. DOS defragmenters know nothing of extended attributes and will not preserve them. Make sure any defragmentation utility you use is guaranteed to work properly with OS/2.

I said there was a risk involved with backing up, erasing your disk then restoring from backup. Be very sure that your backup program is working the way you expect. After you erase your entire disk, it is too late to discover that, due to a procedural error, you *thought* you were backing up, but you really were not.

Test your backup method. Before you entrust your entire hard disk to a backup operation, back up a small, unneeded group of files from your disk, erase them, verify that they are gone, then restore them and verify that they are back. If this test goes well, you can feel reasonably confident that the real procedure will go well.

Just to be safe, make *two* backups before erasing your hard disk. It might not hurt to say a small prayer also.

You are probably asking yourself, "If fragmentation is such a big problem, why did Microsoft and IBM select a file system that is so susceptible to it? Why didn't they choose some other file system that does not have this problem?" The answer goes back to the specifications of the original IBM PC. Fragmentation is no big deal on a floppy disk that only holds 160k. Even with the 320k and later 360k double-sided disks that followed, you couldn't put enough files on a floppy for fragmentation to be much of a factor.

THE EVER-INCREASING NEED FOR MORE DISK SPACE

About the same time the IBM PC was starting its long and successful life, Shugart Technologies (later renamed to Seagate Technologies) delivered the first 5.25-inch form factor hard disk, the 5mb ST-506. The authors of DOS decided that the FAT design would still be viable with such devices, even if they eventually grew to be as large as 30mb. These people didn't believe that personal computers would ever achieve the status of "real" computers. Advanced disk formatting techniques were already being applied to mainframe systems and minicomputers. It was felt that such techniques would be overkill on the PCs of the early 1980s.

The tremendous increase in PC power over the last decade has brought with it a corresponding increase in the magnitude of the jobs people expect from their PCs. Larger, more complex programs and larger data files have led to a steady increase in hard disk capacities. 1 and 2gb models are not uncommon today and have caused the FAT system to become an anachronism.

Many OS/2 users still opt to format one or more of their disk drives with FAT, rather than the more modern HPFS, for reasons of backward compatibility. For well over a decade, personal computer users have been writing programs and creating data on FAT-formatted disks. If IBM wants people to migrate from DOS to OS/2, they must protect their customers' investments by providing a means to use the older programs and data.

Because of a few lingering incompatibilities, some Windows programs will not run under WIN-OS/2 and some DOS programs will not run under OS/2's DOS emulation. For those programs you may wish to install DOS with Windows on your OS/2 machine and put the programs in a partition accessible to both operating systems. We will discuss multiple operating systems later in this chapter. To be accessed by DOS, such programs must be on a FAT-formatted disk.

HPFS

By the time IBM and Microsoft started development of OS/2 2.0, it was clear that the deficiencies of the FAT file system were having a great impact on performance and that the problem would get worse as larger disks became common. In response, the High Performance File System (HPFS) had been developed. It addressed many of the specific areas that were particularly problematic in the FAT system.

Fragmentation was, of course, a big issue. HPFS is designed such that file fragmentation is reduced to negligible proportions. Another problem with FAT systems is *cluster wastage*. A cluster is the smallest addressable unit on a FAT drive. On a small hard disk it might be 2k. On a larger drive it might be 4k or 8k.

If you create a 300-byte file on a large hard disk with 8k clustering, 300 bytes will be used by the file and 7,892 bytes will be wasted. If your work involves the creation of large numbers of small files, the total waste could be significant. The minimum allocation unit under HPFS is 512 bytes. There will still be some waste but a lot less than under FAT.

HPFS files can have names up to 254 characters in length and may contain blank spaces and multiple periods. This gives you considerably more flexibility than the FAT standard 8 characters of filename and three characters of extension with no blanks allowed.

The most frequently accessed portion of any hard disk is the directory, which tells the operating system where files are located on the disk. The FAT system puts the directory on the outermost disk track, making the read/write head do a lot of extra traveling when it is working on files on the inner tracks.

HPFS locates the directory in the middle of the disk, which is where (on the average) the read/write head is located anyway. The reduction in seek time translates into a performance improvement.

Wow! HPFS seems better in every way. Why not format your entire system for HPFS and forget FAT altogether?

 TANSTAAFL. As with all things, there is a price to be paid for the improved performance of HPFS. An extra 500k of RAM is required to maintain a HPFS file system.

If you are tight on memory, stick with FAT. If you have 6mb of RAM or less, forget HPFS.

If your hard disk partition is 60mb or less, stick with FAT. The speed advantages of HPFS (assuming a comparable FAT system is not fragmented) do not become noticeable until your hard disk partition size reaches about 60mb. Why give up 500k of RAM and start swapping earlier if your disk performance will not be improved? Overall performance could *decrease* if you put HPFS on a small partition.

USING MULTIPLE OPERATING SYSTEMS

The DOS operating system allows you to partition a hard disk into as many as four logical drives. Each logical drive is treated as if it were a separate physical device. OS/2 gives you the same option. There are several advantages to this.

1. You could partition your disk into two logical volumes, one FAT and the other HPFS. You could put data that needs to be accessible to both DOS and OS/2 in the FAT partition and OS/2-only material in a large HPFS partition.

2. You could put an entirely unrelated operating system, such as SCO UNIX on the same system with OS/2. Each would have a separate partition and would be completely unaware of the

existence of the other. You get the advantage of running two operating systems, while having to buy only one computer.

3. You could put Microsoft Windows NT in its own partition on the same hard drive with OS/2. Since Windows NT can read and write both FAT and HPFS files, you could share programs and data between OS/2 and Windows NT by creating a third partition accessible to both operating systems.

Before you install OS/2, or any operating system for that matter, you must decide how you are going to partition and format your hard disk (or disks). Under both DOS and OS/2, the utility that does this is FDISK. FDISK is capable of partitioning your hard disk into as many as four volumes. Early in the OS/2 installation procedure you are asked if you want to devote your entire primary hard disk to OS/2. You should know the answer to this question before you start.

Installing OS/2 Only

If OS/2 is the only operating system you will want to run, both now and in the future, you might as well devote your entire hard disk to it. You could divide the disk into a primary partition (C) and an extended partition (D), but there would be no benefit in doing so. You might as well format the drive as one large volume. You must decide whether to format it according to the FAT or the HPFS file system type.

If you are running only OS/2, have more than 6mb of RAM and your disk is larger than 60mb, use HPFS. Compatibility with DOS is a non-issue, you will get better performance than with a FAT file system type and you will not have to worry about fragmentation.

Running Both OS/2 & DOS

If you want to run DOS on your system as well as OS/2—perhaps to run one or more DOS programs that do not run correctly under OS/2's emulation of DOS—you can install OS/2's Dual Boot option. As is true for the OS/2-only case, you can partition your hard disk as a single large volume. If you do, however, you will have to use the FAT file system type. DOS is not capable of using HPFS files.

Another alternative would be to use FDISK to create a primary FAT partition containing both the DOS and OS/2 system files and DOS-specific application files, with an extended HPFS partition that would be accessible only to OS/2.

When you select the Dual Boot option, all your OS/2 system files and all your DOS system files are present in the same primary partition. At boot time you are asked whether you want to boot OS/2 or DOS. Your response determines which system files are invoked and which operating system is activated. To switch operating systems you must reboot by pressing Ctrl+Alt+Del.

Handling More Than Two Operating Systems

You may want to run more than OS/2 2.X and one version of DOS. You may want to run two versions of DOS, say 5.0 and 3.3. You may want to run OS/2 1.1 or 1.2. You may want to run an entirely unrelated operating system, such as SCO UNIX. When you are running OS/2 2.X, you can run up to two other operating systems.

OS/2 handles multiple operating systems on a single system through a utility called Boot Manager. Boot Manager takes control whenever you boot up your system. It lists the operating systems that are installed and asks you which one you want to use. When you enter your selection, it proceeds to load that operating system and then to give it control.

When you install a Boot Manager-based system, use OS/2's FDISK to first create a 1mb primary partition for Boot Manager itself. Then create additional primary partitions for each operating system you want to use. Optionally, you may create an extended partition that is accessible to more than one operating system.

WINDOWS NT

OS/2's closest competitor is Microsoft's Windows NT 3.1, which, like OS/2, is a 32-bit single-user, multithreaded, multitasking operating system. You may want to put NT on the same system as OS/2 for the purpose of making a head-to-head comparison. You may also want to do it because some applications run on OS/2 but not on NT and vice versa.

Boot Manager gives us a mechanism for putting both OS/2 2.X and NT on the same computer. Since OS/2 was not designed with NT in mind and NT was not designed to accommodate OS/2 2.X, making them both work on the same computer is a little tricky. However, by applying a little voodoo here and there you can do it. Success depends to a large extent on doing things in the proper order.

1. Start by doing a normal Boot Manager installation. First install Boot Manager, then OS/2. That will use up two of the four partitions that you may have on a disk.

 Leave plenty of disk space for NT. A full NT installation takes up about 50mb, significantly more than OS/2.

2. Confirm that your OS/2 system is working as it should.

3. Use FDISK to create a partition into which you will install both DOS (preferably version 5.0) and Windows NT.

Avoid DOS 6.0 for this setup. Significant questions about the reliability of DOS 6.0 have been raised, particularly when using the DoubleSpace file compression. Also, the first release of DOS 6.0 disconnects Boot Manager, making your OS/2 partition inaccessible.

4. Set the new partition as Bootable and make it active.

5. Reboot with the DOS Setup Disk and do a normal DOS installation.

6. Do a normal boot. Boot Manager will appear and ask whether you want to boot OS/2 or DOS/NT. Choose DOS/NT. Confirm that DOS is working as it should.

7. Reboot with the NT boot disk and install NT. In the process, NT's boot control program, Flexboot, will be installed.

8. Do a normal boot. Boot Manager will ask whether you want to boot OS/2 or DOS/NT. Choose DOS/NT. Flexboot will appear and ask whether you want to boot Windows NT or DOS. Choose Windows NT. Confirm that NT is working the way it should.

You now have OS/2, DOS and Windows NT all on the same system. Since OS/2 is in one primary partition and both DOS and NT are in another primary partition, they cannot communicate with each other and, in fact, are unaware of each other's existence. Every time you want to switch from one to the other, you must reboot.

Although the OS/2 and Windows NT operating systems on your computer cannot communicate directly, it is possible to set things up so that they can communicate indirectly. Create another partition on the disk (the fourth and last one available). This partition should be an extended partition rather than a primary partition like the other three. An extended partition is accessible to the operating systems running out of any of the boot drive's primary partitions.

Figure 8-4 shows the FDISK screen for a Boot Manager system with OS/2 in one primary partition, DOS and NT in another primary partition and an extended partition that is accessible to both environments.

```
                          FDISK


Disk 1

_____

Partition Information
Name          Status        Access       FS Type        MBytes

_____

              Startable    : Primary    BOOT MANAGER      1
OS2           Bootable     C: Primary    FAT              50
DOS/NT        Bootable     : Primary     FAT              90
              None         D: Logical    FAT              20




_____

F1=Help    F3=Exit        Enter=Options Menu
```

Figure 8-4: The FDISK display of an OS/2 plus NT configuration.

Note that the 1mb Boot Manager partition is marked "Startable."
The OS/2 partition, designated C, is "Bootable" and is of the FAT
type. Since it is only 50mb, there is no advantage to making it HPFS.

The DOS/NT partition is also "Bootable" but does not have a
drive letter assigned to it. This shows that the OS/2 partition is
currently active. When you boot DOS or NT, their partition becomes active and gets the C: drive designation. During that period,
the OS/2 partition does not have a drive letter assigned to it. The
DOS/NT partition is also of the FAT type, since that is the only type
that DOS can use. If NT were in a partition by itself, it could have
either the HPFS type or the NTFS type. The NTFS file system type
works only with NT. OS/2 does not recognize it.

The extended partition, designated D, is a logical drive. Also of
the FAT type, the files it contains can be used by all three operating
systems, DOS, OS/2 and Windows NT.

MOVING ON

You know you are well on the road to mastery of OS/2 voodoo when you have successfully installed OS/2 and it works exactly the way it is supposed to. If you have put it on the same computer with other operating systems and they *all* work the way they are supposed to, you are a true adept.

Now that you can speak with authority about the FAT and the HPFS and such arcane subjects as fragmentation and virtual memory, you are sure to impress everyone at the next cocktail party or witch doctors' convention that you attend.

The next chapter deals with one of the newest and flashiest aspects of personal computing. The multimedia software included with OS/2 allows you to construct sights and sounds that Walt Disney never even dreamed of. Working with what he had, Walt built the Magic Kingdom. Imagine what you will be able to do.

Chapter 9

MULTIMEDIA MAGIC

One of the many definitions of the word "medium" is a channel of communication. The word "multimedia" implies multiple channels of communication working together to convey complex information to multiple senses. If you can supply reinforcing messages to two or more senses at the same time, the impact of that combined message will be multiplied. This is why television grew from laboratory curiosity to indispensable appliance in virtually every household in America in the space of a single generation. Now, anywhere you find electricity, you will find television. By delivering both pictures and sound, television is a multimedia communications device.

In computer circles, the word multimedia has come to take on a more restricted meaning. Multimedia is the delivery of *computer-based* information to users through two or more sensory channels. Computer information has traditionally been delivered visually, through static text or graphics on a screen or in a printed report. Multimedia systems add new dimensions to information delivery. When you add sound or motion to a visual image, communication is enhanced. Any time you use more than one pathway to the user's brain to deliver computer-based information, you are using multimedia.

AUDIO

If you could add only one new channel of information to those traditionally provided on personal computers, sound would probably be the overwhelming choice. Sight is the highest bandwidth input channel humans have, which is why it has been the chief mode of conveying information to users since the beginning of computers. Hearing is the next richest means of communicating. Sound can contain incredible nuances through volume, pitch, timbre, resonance, rhythm and through changes of these qualities over time. Many would contend that sound is more effective at touching human emotions than is sight.

In view of its power, it is not surprising that sound was the first multimedia capability added to the Apple Macintosh, a machine that has done much of the pioneering in multimedia. Now, IBM-compatible PCs have excellent potential as multimedia machines through the addition of sound cards available from a number of vendors.

MIDI (Musical Instrument Digital Interface) is a standard developed in the early 1980s that specifies the format and physical interfaces for the transmission of music from one digital electronic device to another. Nowadays, most composers and professional performers who use electronic instruments use MIDI. It has become the *lingua franca* of the music world.

With MIDI, you can convey an entire musical score, including multiple instruments, each playing multiple notes, from one device to another. For example, you could play a song into a MIDI keyboard, connected by MIDI cable to your computer. In the computer, sequencer software could transform the messages coming from the keyboard into a score that you could then annotate and print. Conversely, music stored in the computer could be sent to one or more instruments and played.

MIDI is a boon to composers who are not great performers. You can compose and score a song, then hear how it sounds when played correctly, even if you can't play it yourself. MIDI synthesizers can generate the sounds of up to 128 melodic and 47 percussive instruments.

⚡ *TRAP* **MIDI only supports 16 sound tracks at a time.** If you want to score and then listen to a composition for a 75-piece orchestra accompanied by a mighty pipe organ, you will have to do it in chunks. Various synthesizers may be even more restrictive in the maximum number of notes they can play at once and the maximum number of different instruments they can simulate at a time.

VIDEO

Although the visual representation of text and graphics on personal computers has been taken for granted for years, animation and movies are relatively new. This is largely due to the fact that moving images, like audio, require a tremendous amount of storage. Until recently, the cost of storage has kept video out of the hands of the average PC user. The cost of storage—including RAM, disk and optical—has declined steadily since personal computers were introduced in the mid-1970s. That lower cost now makes it feasible to support both audio and video on moderately priced machines.

By combining movies, either computer-generated or taken with a video camera, with audio sounds and the more traditional text and graphics, a computer presentation can deliver a message with far more impact than would be possible with a static display on a screen.

As the price of storage continues to decline, it will be possible to store more minutes of larger images of higher resolution and more colors. Computerized video will become feasible for a wide range of information presentation applications. This is a good thing to start learning now, for it is certain to become more important soon.

PLAYING A MULTIMEDIA PRODUCTION

The two principal multimedia activities are creating or *authoring* a multimedia production and viewing or *playing* one. Authoring a multimedia production can be a very involved process, requiring expensive equipment and considerable expertise. Some types of multimedia production can be done, however, with a basic multimedia PC by a person with an interest and the time to experiment.

Playing multimedia objects that already exist (sounds, music, movies) is easy and requires little in the way of special hardware.

Hardware

Much of the hardware that you need to play multimedia presentations is already present with any computer that can run OS/2. Remember that multimedia is a big consumer of both disk storage and system memory. The more you have of both, the better your machine will perform as a multimedia PC.

The ordinary computer's main deficiency (from the multimedia standpoint) is in sound production. It is able to emit beeps out of a low quality speaker, and that is about it. To upgrade an ordinary PC into a multimedia PC, you will need to add a sound card and some decent speakers.

There are a number of sound cards on the market. OS/2 currently supports the IBM M-Audio Capture and Playback Adapter, several models of Creative Labs's Sound Blaster board and Media Vision's Pro AudioSpectrum 16 board. Support for other sound cards is constantly being added both by IBM and vendors. When you are shopping for a sound board, make sure it is supported by OS/2.

If you have a stereo system, you should be able to run your sound output through its amplifier and speakers. If you already have these components, using them for multimedia as well as entertainment costs you nothing.

After a sound board, the most useful hardware component you can buy is a CD-ROM drive. You do not need a CD-ROM drive to play multimedia, but it sure helps. A single CD-ROM disk can hold over 500mb of information. Since both sound and movie files are notoriously large, it is much more convenient for suppliers to deliver them on CD-ROM than on floppy disks.

IBM delivers OS/2 2.1 on either floppy disks or CD-ROM. If you get the CD-ROM version, a large selection of movie files and sound files are included that are not present on the floppies.

Purchase a CD-ROM drive if you intend to do any serious multimedia work.

Not all CD-ROM drives on the market are compatible with OS/2. When shopping for a CD-ROM drive, make sure that you can get OS/2 drivers for it. Drivers are small programs that provide an interface between an operating system and a peripheral device. Many, but not all, of the popular brands of CD-ROM are supported by drivers that come with OS/2.

If you can afford it, get a double-speed CD-ROM drive. A standard CD-ROM drive has a data transfer rate of 150,000 bytes per second. A double-speed drive can transfer data at twice that speed. If you want to run movies directly off the CD-ROM, the double-speed drive will do a much better job. There will be fewer distracting hesitations, as the display waits for images to come in from the CD-ROM.

You will get the best display by copying your movie file to hard disk and running it from there. Even a double-speed drive will not be able to keep up with the data transfer requirements of a 320x240 pixel image in 256 colors at 24 frames per second (normal movie speed). To do this for a one minute movie, however, you will need to have about fifteen megabytes of free disk space.

Buy an OS/2-compatible CD-ROM drive and use it for music as well as for computer storage. If you have not yet added a compact disk player to your entertainment complex, you can kill two birds with one stone. OS/2 includes software that allows you to run your CD-ROM drive as if it were a music CD player. It accepts ordinary music CDs and, when played through your entertainment system's amplifier and speakers, has the same sound quality as a premium music CD player.

Software

OS/2 includes all the software you need to get started in multimedia. Although the IBM Multimedia Presentation Manager/2 (MMPM/2) contains some authoring capability, it is primarily aimed at playing multimedia-ware rather than at creating it. IBM and other vendors have software with more advanced authoring capabilities.

Installing MMPM/2

Even though MMPM/2 is present on your OS/2 installation disks or CD-ROM, it is not installed with the standard OS/2 installation. You must install it in a separate operation using a different installation program. To install MMPM/2 you need a minimum of 8mb of system memory. You also need 5mb of hard disk space to hold the MMPM/2 files.

 The above stated requirements are _bare_ minimums. The more you have of both system memory and disk space, the better.

You can play software motion video, also known as digital video, without any additional hardware (other than memory) beyond what is required for OS/2 itself. Digital audio, however, including the sound that goes along with a digital video movie, requires that an OS/2-compatible sound card be present in the system.

The following software installation procedures for MMPM/2 assume that sufficient memory, disk space and a sound card are already installed, tested and verified to be functioning.

INSTALLING FROM FLOPPY DISKS

1. Insert the first MMPM/2 installation disk into your A drive.

2. Open the Drive A icon on the OS/2 desktop.

3. Select MINSTALL.EXE and click on OK. The MMPM/2 logo window will appear.

4. Proceed to Common Installation Procedure.

INSTALLING FROM CD-ROM OR A NETWORK

1. Start an OS/2 full-screen or OS/2 window session.

2. Change the current drive to the drive you are installing from (either CD-ROM or network).

3. Change to the MMPM2 subdirectory.

4. Type MINSTALL then Enter. The MMPM/2 logo window will appear.

5. Proceed to Common Installation Procedure.

COMMON INSTALLATION PROCEDURE

1. Select OK or press the Enter key. The multimedia installation window will appear (Figure 9-1).

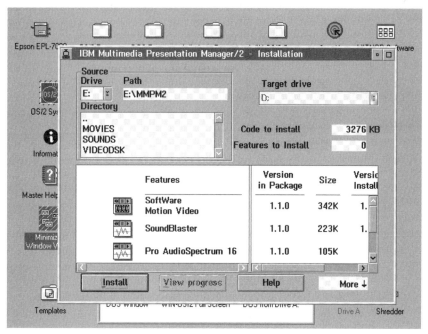

Figure 9-1: The MMPM/2 Installation window.

2. Verify that the source drive and path are correct and that the target drive is the one you want to place the files on. If any of these items is incorrect, adjust it before proceeding.

3. The Code to install field shows that 3,276k of code is to be installed before any features are added. To get MMPM/2 to do anything, you must add features. Add whichever features you want within your memory limits.

4. After you have selected the appropriate sound board, Software Motion Video and CD Audio, click on the Install button.

5. MINSTALL will automatically update your CONFIG.SYS file, if you consent. If you do not, you must update it manually to include new drivers. The new command lines will be included in a file named CONFIGCH.NEW. Use it as a model for changing CONFIG.SYS.

6. After CONFIG.SYS is modified, you must reboot so the changes can take effect. Do a normal shutdown of OS/2, then reboot. When the OS/2 desktop appears, it should have the Multimedia and Volume Control icons on it. Its appearance should also be heralded by a short trumpet solo and the sound of an electronic window opening up.

What If You Don't Get Sound After Installation?

Although installing MMPM/2 software is fairly straightforward, installing the hardware is not. There are a number of things that, if not done properly, will result in either partial sound or no sound at all. Check the following possibilities:

1. Make sure the sound board you installed is compatible with OS/2, and that the proper device driver is installed in your CONFIG.SYS file.

2. Boot up from DOS and see if the sound card functions correctly under DOS. If it does not, your problem is not an OS/2 problem.

3. Verify that all the connections between your sound card, your amplifier and your speakers are correct. Make sure that the amplifier and speakers work properly with another sound source, such as your tape deck or FM radio.

4. Make sure that your amplifier source selection switch is in the proper position to receive signals from your sound card. Try all the others too, just in case.

5. Sound cards may be installed with one of several I/O addresses, interrupt request lines and DMA channels. The ones you pick cannot conflict with other installed devices.

   Typically the I/O address, IRQ line and DMA channel for a sound board are set by the placement of jumpers on the board. Examine the jumpers closely in conjunction with the board's documentation to determine how they are set. Next, examine the jumpers (or run the software setup programs) for all the other devices in your computer and determine what their I/O addresses, IRQ lines and DMA channels are. If one of the settings on your sound card conflicts with one of your existing devices, change the sound card to a non-conflicting setting.

6. You may still have problems after doing everything listed above. Subtle interactions among your sound board, the sound board's device driver, the MMPM/2 software, your computer's system board and other boards installed in your system could cause intermittent or solid problems. If this happens, isolate the problem as much as possible. Take out all non-essential expansion boards. Run under DOS rather than OS/2. If you still have a problem, document it carefully. Look for advice on CompuServe, then call your sound board's BBS or technical support line.

Digital Audio Media Player

The Digital Audio Media Player is an application that plays, records and edits digital audio files. The functions of playing and recording sounds are very similar to the playing and recording of sounds with an ordinary cassette tape player. The function of editing sounds is similar to that performed by equipment in a professional sound studio. To put all three functions into familiar terms, the Digital Audio Media Player can be displayed two ways. For playback and recording, it looks like the control panel of a tape recorder. For editing, it looks like a sophisticated piece of studio equipment.

PLAYING A SOUND

To play an existing sound file, you want the Player/Recorder view of the application. This is the default, so you do not need to pull down the View menu to select it. Figure 9-2 shows the Player/Recorder view of the Digital Audio application on the desktop.

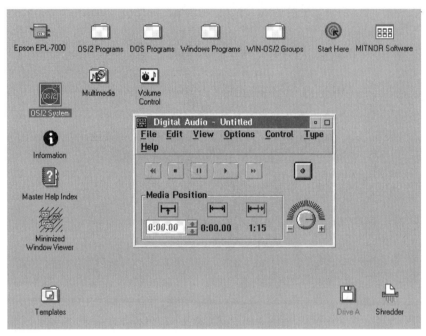

Figure 9-2: Player/Recorder view of Digital Audio application.

As yet, no sound file has been selected, so the normal player function buttons in the center (rewind, stop, pause, play and fast forward) are grayed out. The record button with a red dot in its center is enabled, since you do not need a loaded sound file to start a recording session.

To play an existing sound, you must pull down the file menu and select Open. The dialog box shown in Figure 9-3 will appear on the screen. If it is not looking at the drive and directory where your sound files are stored, select the proper directory. Then select one of your existing .WAV files by double-clicking on it.

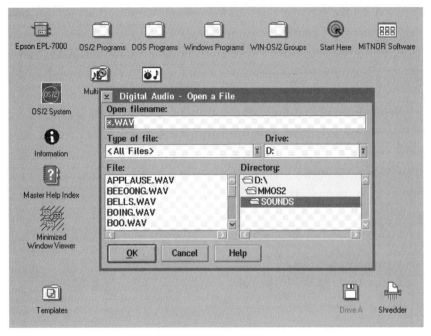

Figure 9-3: The Open a File dialog box.

If you click on the Play button now, the selected sound will be played from your speakers. You can hit the Play button repeatedly; the sound will be played every time.

You can use the Control menu instead. If you forget what the symbols on top of the buttons mean or just do not care for pushing simulated buttons, the Control menu has text equivalents of all the recorder function buttons.

Control the volume. When you first call up the media player, the volume control located in the lower right corner is cranked up to full volume. You can control the volume by clicking on the minus sign to lower it or the plus sign to raise it.

The Media Position box shows the progress of the sound file you are playing. For sound bites that only last a second or two, this is of limited value. By the time you see the numbers change, the performance is over.

RECORDING A SOUND

Recording a sound is a little more complicated than playing one. You must decide where the input sound will come from: either a microphone or a line coming from some other device such as a radio, TV, cassette player or CD player. Also specify what volume level to expect the input signal to have and whether to feed it to your speakers while it is being recorded. These choices are made from the Options menu.

Next, you must tell the media player whether to record in monophonic or stereophonic mode, what sampling rate to use and what quality level to use (Figure 9-4). The choices you make here have a significant effect on how much memory your recorded sound will consume.

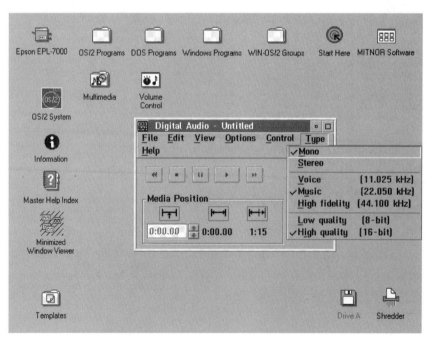

Figure 9-4: The media player Type menu.

Stereo sound takes up more disk space than Mono. If you are recording sounds with a single microphone, choose Mono to save disk space.

In digital recording, the sampling rate should be at least twice the highest frequency you expect the input signal to carry. If it is any less, the fidelity of the recorded sound suffers. A sampling rate of 11.025 KHz is good enough for voice, which falls into a relatively narrow frequency band around 3 KHz. For music of portable radio quality, a sampling rate of 22.050 Khz is sufficient. To match the quality of a high fidelity home music system, 44.100 KHz is required. Of course, if you double the sampling rate, you increase the amount of disk space needed to hold the recorded sound. Some boards feature hardware real-time data compression, which reduces the amount of disk space needed.

Select the lowest sampling rate that still satisfies your sound quality requirements. You will thus use the least amount of disk space.

Most sound boards available today are 8-bit boards that have an 8-bit wide path from the sound board to your system bus and your memory. An 8-bit board gives you about 48 dB of dynamic range, which is about the same as that of an average cassette deck. Dynamic range is the difference between the loudest and the softest sounds that can be produced. Some more recent and more expensive sound boards, such as the Sound Blaster Pro 16 ASP and the Pro Audio Spectrum 16, have a 16-bit-wide data path. These boards provide 96 dB of dynamic range, which is about the same as the quality you get from CDs.

Select a quality type appropriate for your board and disk space. If you have an 8-bit board, select Low quality. It will not do you any good to select High quality, since your board does not support it. If you have a 16-bit board, you may select High quality. If you select Low quality instead, the sound quality of your recording will be reduced, as will be the amount of space it occupies on disk.

SYSTEM SOUNDS

System sounds are digital audio sound bytes associated with various system events. For example, one sound is associated with the opening of a window and plays every time a window on the desktop is opened. A different sound is associated with the closing of a window. In all, thirteen system events can be associated with a sound. The default sounds range from under a second to two seconds in duration.

Each sound is contained in a digital audio (.WAV) file. You can create your own .WAV files with the Digital Audio Media Player application, using its Recorder function. You could then associate your own custom sound effects with the system events on your OS/2 desktop or within an application.

Figure 9-5 shows the System Sounds settings notebook. The Sound page shows a list of system events, a list of sound files that can be associated with them, a volume control knob and a Play button. To hear how a particular .WAV file sounds, select <Try it> in the System events window, select the desired file in the Sound file window then press the Play button. The selected sound will be played through the speakers connected to your sound board.

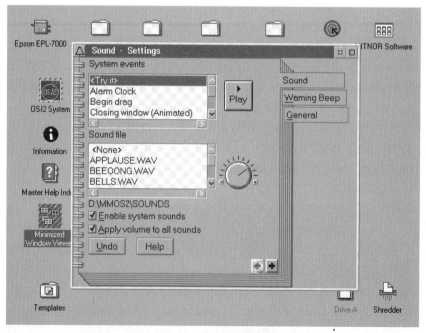

Figure 9-5: The System Sounds settings notebook Sound page.

Only one application may use the audio device at a time. Thus if you have left the Digital Audio Media Player open on the desktop, even if it is minimized and invisible, the System Sounds application will not play the .WAV file that you select, or anything else for that matter. As long as the Digital Audio Media Player is active, none of the system sounds will be audible.

The .WAV files provided with OS/2 are good-quality sound effects, but they are all rather short and generalized. When you create your own .WAV files, you can incorporate them into the system sounds, making your work environment as personal as you like.

For example, one of the events that you can associate a sound with is system startup. The default sound file is a rousing but short trumpet solo named CHARGE.WAV. You can record your own startup sound with the media player then associate it with the system startup event.

Say your top systems analyst is named Dave. As his supervisor you might record a message such as "Good morning, Dave. You'll get a lot done today." Name the file GREET.WAV, then use the System Sounds setup notebook to replace CHARGE.WAV with GREET.WAV. Now every time Dave boots up his computer in the morning, he will hear your cheerful voice greeting and encouraging him. This will doubtless brighten his day and cause him to perform better. It will also repeatedly deliver the message to his subconscious that you care about him and take a personal interest in his work. Of course, if Dave is a cynic by nature, this idea may have the reverse effect. Use your own judgment.

EDITING A SOUND

The Digital Audio Media Player gives you tools to edit sounds stored in .WAV files. You can modify the existing sounds that come with OS/2 or new ones that you create. Figure 9-6 shows the Edit view of the Digital Audio Media Player. It is larger than the Player/Recorder view and has more functions. In the figure, the digital audio file GREET.WAV has been loaded. A visual representation of the waveform is displayed across the bottom of the window.

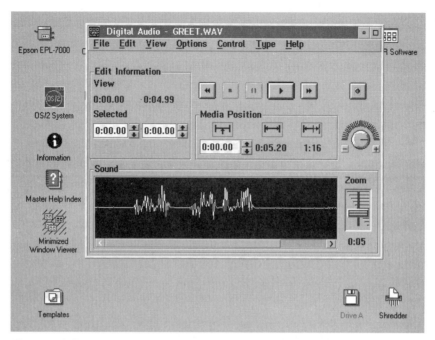

Figure 9-6: The Edit view of Digital Audio Media Player.

The middle number in the media position box shows that the entire sound clip is 5.20 seconds long. It is clear from the waveform that much of that time is dead space at the beginning and the end of the file. Since silence occupies just as much disk space as sound does, it would be helpful to cut out the silent stretches at the beginning and end of the file.

Before you can perform an editing operation, you must mark the portion of the sound file that you want to work on. Do that by putting the mouse pointer on the beginning of the area of interest and dragging it to the end of the area of interest. In our case, start at the beginning of the Sound window and drag until just before the waveform starts deviating from the zero line. The area marked will be highlighted in a different color (Figure 9-7).

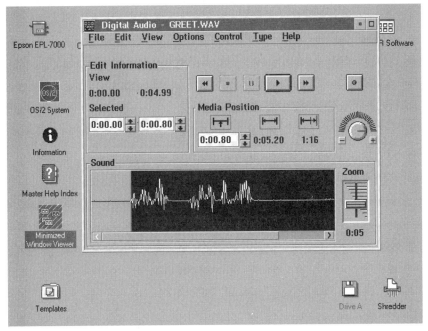

Figure 9-7: The silent stretch at the beginning of the sound file is marked.

To edit the marked area, pull down the edit menu (Figure 9-8).

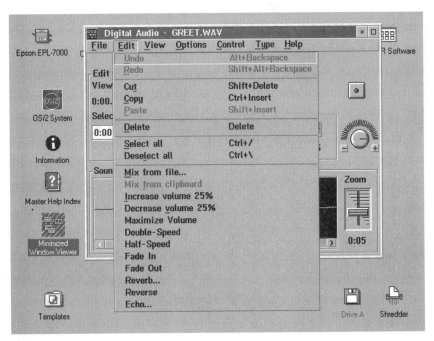

Figure 9-8: The Edit menu.

There are a number of things you can do with the waveform contained in the highlighted area.

- You can Cut it out of this file to the Clipboard and from there paste it into another .WAV file.

- You can Copy it from this file to the Clipboard, without affecting this file.

- You can mix it with a sound from another file.

- You can increase or decrease the volume level by 25%.

- You can put the pedal to the metal with Maximize Volume.

- By selecting Double-Speed you can halve the playing time while doubling the pitch of the sounds. This is great for making Alvin and the Chipmunks recordings.

- By selecting Half-Speed you can double the playing time while halving the pitch. This is great for doing imitations of HAL-9000 just before Dave extracts HAL's last memory module.

- Fade In, Fade Out, Reverb and Echo are nifty studio effects.

- Reverse will play your sound file backward. This is a highly effective means of surreptitiously implanting counterculture ideas into the minds of impressionable youths.

All these options are great fun, but for our current purposes we want the Delete option. When you select it, the stretch of silence at the beginning is removed. Do the same to the silence at the end of the file. Figure 9-9 shows the result. The edited file has been reduced almost in half.

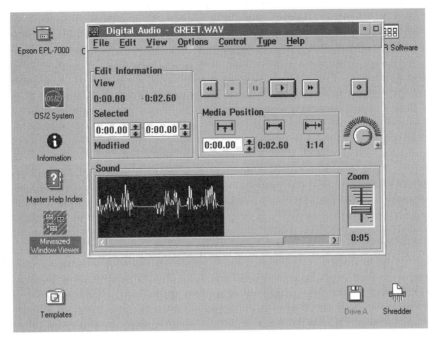

Figure 9-9: GREET.WAV after deletion of silent stretches.

Don't get carried away creating a lot of lengthy sound files.
Even though it has been shortened, GREET.WAV still takes up about four times as much disk space as does CHARGE.WAV. If running short of disk space is a concern of yours, as it always is for me, keep only sound files that you regularly use. Archive the rest to floppy or tape.

You can include the playing of a sound in your own programs.
An undocumented file, PLAY.CMD, included with OS/2, will play any .WAV file you specify. PLAY.CMD is located in your MMOS2 directory and has the following syntax:

```
PLAY [FILE=filename][DEV=device][TIMEFMT=timefmt]
[FROM=from_position][TO=to_position]
```

The FILE and DEV parameters are mandatory and the others are optional. To include the GREET.WAV sound file in a program you could include a command similar to the following:

```
PLAY FILE=d:\mmos2\sounds\greet.wav DEV=waveaudio01
```

Waveaudio01 is the device type of the digital audio circuitry on my Sound Blaster Pro 16 ASP. Your device type may differ. To find out the device type of your digital audio circuit, open the Digital Audio Media Player's settings notebook. The Program tab will show Required path and file name and Optional Parameters. The device type of your digital audio circuit should be displayed in the Optional Parameters field (Figure 9-10).

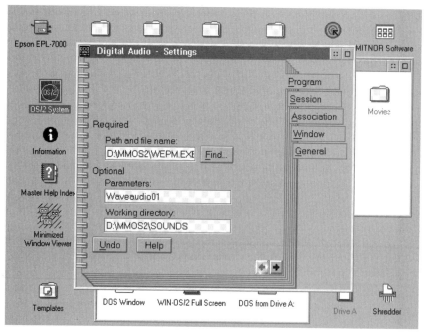

Figure 9-10: The Settings notebook shows device type as an Optional Parameter.

 You can also play a sound from the desktop by clicking on its icon. Use the following procedure:

1. Open the OS/2 System Editor.

2. Enter the command,

```
PLAY FILE=d:\mmos2\sounds\greet.wav DEV=waveaudio01
```

Note: Use your own .WAV filename and your own device type in the expression shown above.

3. Save the file as GREET.CMD.

4. Find the icon for GREET.CMD in the folder corresponding to the directory you saved it to.

5. Double-click on the GREET.CMD icon. An OS/2 command prompt window will open. GREET.CMD will execute in it. You will hear the message. After program completion, the window will disappear.

MIDI Media Player

The MIDI Media Player is an application with rather limited functionality. Its main purpose is to play MIDI files that already exist. To create your own MIDI files, you will need hardware not normally included in a sound board and software other than that supplied with OS/2. To play a MIDI file, open the MIDI application to display the Player (Figure 9-11).

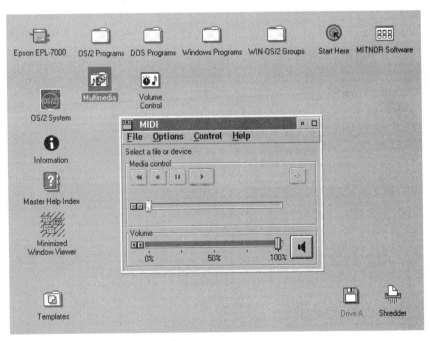

Figure 9-11: MIDI Media Player.

MIDI files take up much less disk space than digital audio files for the same amount of music. A digital audio .WAV file contains a snapshot of the sound waveform, a veritable bitmap of sound. For high fidelity this requires huge amounts of disk space. Even for low fidelity it requires a lot. MIDI files, on the other hand, do not contain a representation of the sound. Instead, they contain performance information such as note on, note off, velocity, pressure, pitch and program changes. This performance information is sent to a synthesizer, which recreates the music from the information.

MIDI is best for long pieces of high-quality instrumental music. It cannot convey speech.

Digital audio is best for brief sound effects and voice. It can reproduce any sound but uses large amounts of disk space in the process.

Digital Video Media Player

Perhaps the highest form of multimedia production is the combination of high fidelity stereophonic sound with high resolution, full motion video. Digital video technology is still in its infancy at the PC level. The processing power of current personal computers is almost, but not quite, good enough to present a professional-quality digital video presentation.

Get involved with digital video and become knowledgeable. Even though current PC hardware is not fast enough and does not have enough memory to produce and display quality digital video, these obstacles will soon disappear. PC performance continues to improve at a rapid rate. Within two years PCs will be able to support very good quality presentations incorporating digital video. If you learn about it now, you will be ahead of the crowd.

OS/2's Digital Video Media Player, like the MIDI Media Player, is a very basic application. All it does is play back digital video (.AVI) files. Microsoft developed the Audio Video Interleaved (AVI) technology to allow the creation, editing and presentation of digitized motion in a window on the computer screen. As its name implies, the moving video is synchronized with a sound track. Both the sound and visual information are contained in the .AVI file.

Get the CD-ROM version of OS/2 2.1 rather than the version delivered on floppy disks. If you are interested in multimedia, you will need the large storage capacity of a CD-ROM anyway. The floppy disk version of OS/2 2.1 contains only one small clip of a single .AVI file, recorded in the smallest format (160x120 pixels). In contrast, the CD-ROM version contains a large selection of .AVI files in two different formats, IBM Ultimotion and Intel Indeo. Files in the 320x240 format are included as well as those with 160x120 pixels. Run times are longer and a choice of either 8-bit or 16-bit audio is given. With the sample files on the CD-ROM, you can get a good idea of what is possible with the technology.

Bandwidth is the number of bits per second of signal that pass through a communications channel. Digital video requires more bandwidth than a PC has. To make up for this deficiency, various tricks are used to allow PCs to play digital video. These tricks are streaming, image compression, frame rate and frame skipping.

OS/2's digital video media player uses a technique called *streaming* to transfer the images and sound from the storage device (either CD-ROM or hard disk) to the computer's screen and speakers. Bytes of data from the .AVI file are flowed from the storage device directly to the processor in a continuous stream rather than being routed to the computer's memory first. The extra operation of going through memory (the normal way of running programs) would slow things down and introduce hesitations in the display.

Even with streaming, the transfer rate of CD-ROM drives and even hard disk drives is not high enough to keep up with the display rate of normal video. Normal TV quality video is displayed at 30 frames per second (fps). Normal theatrical movies are displayed at 24 fps.

To display a 320x240 window showing 256 colors and running at 24 fps requires a transfer rate of over 1.8 million bytes per second. Today's fastest, so-called double-speed CD-ROM drives have a transfer rate of 300 thousand bytes per second. Less expensive normal-speed drives have a 150 thousand byte per second transfer rate. Hard disks are faster but still not fast enough. To make digital video possible, *image compression* is used. Since only a little of the image changes from one frame to the next in a movie, instead of sending the entire frame all the time, only the differences between the previous frame and the current one are sent. This dramatically reduces the bandwidth required, making the illusion of motion possible.

Another way of reducing required bandwidth is to send video frames at a lower *frame rate*. Fifteen frames per second still provides a good simulation of smooth motion, although a slight jerkiness is detectable. The advantage is a substantial reduction in the number of bytes that must be transferred per second.

Even with all the techniques mentioned above, current reasonably priced hardware cannot keep up a 24 or even a 15 fps display rate for movies with a lot of detail. Movies with high complexity do not compress well. In order to keep these movies synchronized with the sound track, *frame skipping* is employed when a delay in transmission causes one frame to freeze momentarily on the screen while the storage device catches up. If frame skipping becomes too pronounced, important information is lost.

 If you use digital video, be sure your screen mode is at least 640x480x256. Sixteen color video looks terrible, and MMP-MP/2 does not support it.

 Invest in a double-speed CD-ROM drive. Performance from a 150k/second drive is unacceptable for digital video.

 Copy your .AVI file from CD-ROM to hard disk before viewing it. The motion will be much more realistic.

Be sure your disk is not fragmented. Fragmented disks are much slower and digital video is one place where the difference really shows up.

 If you have enough RAM (16mb or more), create a virtual disk in RAM and copy your .AVI file to it before playing it. This will give you the most realistic motion of all. The syntax to load a device driver for a 2mb virtual disk in your CONFIG.SYS file is:

```
DEVICE=C:\OS2\VDISK.SYS 2048 512 64
```

Sector size is 512 bytes and a maximum of 64 directory entries may be made on the new virtual drive. This statement should appear *after* all the other drivers that set up your disk devices.

 Your RAM-depleted system will start swapping sooner. A virtual disk in RAM large enough to hold an .AVI file that runs for several seconds can slow down such things as window opening and file loading.

 Use a smaller video window if you can. Remember that a 320x240 window contains four times as many picture elements as does a 160x120 window. All other things being equal, four times as much data must be transmitted per second to play a 320x240 movie as is needed for a 160x120 movie.

 To generate you own .AVI files, you will need to buy additional hardware and software.

IBM provides two different implementations of software motion video with OS/2 2.1, their own Ultimotion and Intel's Indeo. Sample files that play at 24, 15 and 5 fps are provided in both 320x240 and 160x120 formats. Some have 16-bit sound on their sound tracks and others have 8-bit sound. By looking at various versions of the same clip, you can determine what constitutes satisfactory video and audio for you. Ultimotion supports 65,000 colors as well as 256. There are no 65,000 color sample files on the OS/2 2.1 CD-ROM. Video boards that support 65,000 colors are generally more expensive than the standard 256 color boards. 65,000 color video starts to approach the quality of photographic film when combined with a sufficiently high-resolution display.

Compact Disc Application

The Compact Disc application included with OS/2's multimedia tools allows you to get double duty out of your CD-ROM player. You can use it to play standard audio CDs as well as data-laden CD-ROMs. If you are running your sound output through a good quality amplifier to good quality speakers, you can play your favorite music CDs as background music while you work on other applications. Since OS/2 is a multitasking operating system, you can do this as long as you are not using digital audio or MIDI.

If you have an external amplifier, CD output does not need to be routed through your sound board. If you are not going to do any computer processing of the sound, go directly to the amplifier for best reproduction. Since this signal is entering the amplifier through a different input port than the one used by your sound board, you will have to switch to a new source on your amplifier's front panel to hear CD music.

Figure 9-12 shows the virtual front panel of your CD player.

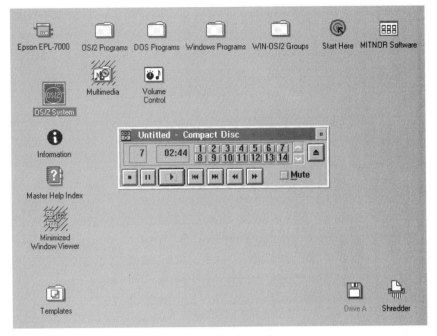

Figure 9-12: The Compact Disc player front panel.

The panel shows the number of the track currently being played and the current position on that track in minutes and seconds. To the right are selection buttons you can use to select a specific track to play next. Buttons along the bottom of the panel perform standard functions:

- Stop playing
- Pause toggle
- Play current track
- Go to beginning of track, or if already at beginning, go to previous track
- Go to next track
- Move backward in current track
- Move forward in current track

The button at the right with a triangle pointing up is the electronic eject button for drives that support electronic eject. The Mute check box in the lower right is a toggle to disable and reenable the playing of sound. If you run the audio output directly from your CD-ROM drive to your external amplifier, the Mute toggle will have no effect.

You can disable the playing of selected tracks. Press and hold the Shift key while clicking on the unwanted track number with mouse button 1.

By clicking on the menu widget in the upper left corner of the CD player window, you can pull down a menu that gives you even more control over operations than do the front panel buttons. The Control option on this menu leads to a submenu that encompasses all of the front panel functions. In addition, the Options choice leads to a submenu with some new functions (Figure 9-13).

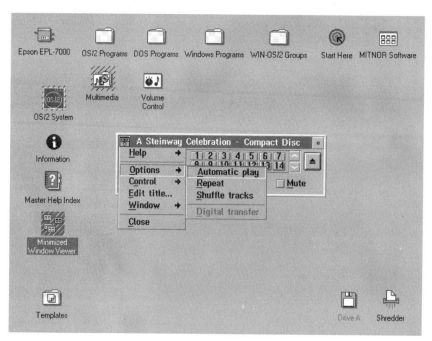

Figure 9-13: The Compact Disc player front panel Options submenu.

If Automatic play is selected, a compact disc will start playing as soon as you put it into the CD-ROM device. When you select Repeat, the player will automatically replay the CD that has just finished playing in the same track order and with the same tracks disabled. When you select the Shuffle tracks toggle, the tracks of the current CD will be played in random order. If you select it again, the order will return to normal.

The Edit title... choice on the menu gives you the opportunity to identify the CD that is currently in the player. Once you enter a title, the legend "Untitled" in the title bar is replaced with your new title. The player application remembers this information; the next time the same CD is inserted in the player, its proper title will appear in the title bar.

When you reinsert a CD that you have played previously, the player will remember not only its title but also what tracks were disabled last time. Those same tracks will be disabled again and will not play.

The Windows option on the menu has all the standard window choices, such as maximize, minimize and restore. It also has the choices Default size and Compact size. If you want to keep control of the player (which you can't do if you minimize it), but still devote a minimum of screen real estate to it, choose Compact size. Everything will disappear except the title bar and the control buttons. To redisplay the full player face plate, choose Default size.

Multimedia Data Converter

Since multimedia is still a young field, there is not much standardization yet. There are a number of different file formats for still video, motion video and audio. Macintosh formats are different from Windows and OS/2 formats. This will likely change in the future. In the meantime there must be some way of converting files from one format to another. OS/2's Multimedia Data converter converts several of the most popular formats in use on IBM-compatible PCs. Macintosh formats are not currently supported.

TO SUMMARIZE

Multimedia is an emerging technology comparable to PC technology in the late 1970s. Since then, PC technology has become a multi-billion-dollar industry; its effects are felt throughout our society. Multimedia could grow to have a similar importance. Knowledge of and experience with multimedia will have strong market value. Consider any time and money that you invest in multimedia now to be an investment in your own future. Since MMPM/2 comes "free" with OS/2 2.1, your investment will be small indeed compared to the possible payoff.

INDEX

Colophon

This book was produced using Aldus PageMaker 5.0 on a 486 PC clone with 16mb of RAM. The video system is a Cornerstone DualPage 120 grayscale monitor driven by an ImageExcel controller. Pages were proofed on a LaserWriter Pro 630. Final output was produced on film using a Linotronic 330.

Screen images were captured using the PrntScrn utility from MITNOR Software. The body copy is set in TrueType Galliard and Switzerland Black Condensed. Display copy is set in Digital Typeface Corporation's Dom Casual and Tribecca.

WORK WONDERS WITH VENTANA VOODOO!

VOODOO DOS, SECOND EDITION
$21.95
277 pages, illustrated
ISBN: 1-56604-046-9
Updated for all versions of DOS through 6.0, *Voodoo Dos, Second Edition*, offers a wide range of time-saving techniques designed for all users. You'll find a wealth of help for customization; using the DOS editor; working with Shell and more! Learn to streamline time-consuming tasks and maximize your DOS productivity!

VOODOO MAC
$21.95
340 pages, illustrated
ISBN: 1-56604-028-0
Whether you're a power user or a beginner, *Voodoo Mac* has something for everyone! Computer veteran Kay Nelson has compiled hundreds of invaluable tips, tricks, hints and shortcuts that simplify your Macintosh tasks and save time, including disk and drive magic, fonta and printing tips, alias alchemy and more!

VOODOO WINDOWS

$19.95
282 pages, illustrated
ISBN: 1-56604-005-1

A unique resource, *Voodoo Windows* bypasses the obtuse technical information found in many Windows books to bring you an abundance of never-before-published tips, tricks and shortcuts for maximum Windows productivity. A one-of-a-kind reference for beginners and experienced users alike.

VOODOO WINDOWS NT

$24.95
385 pages, illustrated
ISBN: 1-56604-069-8

Discover a cauldron of creative advice for mastering Microsoft's powerful new 32-bit operating system! A wealth of techniques for streamlining your work and increasing productivity is at your fingertips with time-saving tips, tricks and shortcuts for a variety of tasks. You'll find hundreds of hints for simplifying your NT tasks without having to wade through obtuse technical information.

VOODOO NETWARE

$27.95
315 pages, illustrated
ISBN: 1-56604-077-9

Overcome network computing obstacles with insightful tips, tricks and shortcuts from *Voodoo NetWare*. This unique guide offers network managers an unparalleled collection of advice for troubleshooting, increasing user productivity and streamlining NetWare tasks. NetWare 4.0 users will find timely tips for a variety of commands and features.

For faster service, order toll-free 800/743-5369.
Ventana Press, P.O. Box 2468, Chapel Hill, NC 27515 (919) 942-0220; Fax: (919) 942-1140

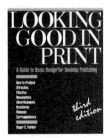

TO ORDER additional copies of *Voodoo OS/2* or any other Ventana Press title, please fill out this order form and return it to us for quick shipment. Ask about other books in the Ventana Voodoo™ Series!

	Quantity	Price	Total
Voodoo OS/2	_____	x $24.95 =	$_____
Voodoo NetWare	_____	x $27.95 =	$_____
Voodoo Mac	_____	x $21.95 =	$_____
Voodoo Windows	_____	x $19.95 =	$_____
Voodoo DOS, Second Edition	_____	x $21.95 =	$_____
Ventana Voodoo™ Series Library (all 5 Voodoo books)	_____	x $81.75 =	$_____
Desktop Publishing With WordPerfect— Windows Edition	_____	x $21.95 =	$_____
Desktop Publishing With WordPerfect 6	_____	x $24.95 =	$_____
Desktop Publishing With Word for Windows	_____	x $21.95 =	$_____
Looking Good in Print, Third Edition	_____	x $24.95 =	$_____
Visual Guide to Visual Basic, Second Edition	_____	x $29.95 =	$_____
Windows, Word & Excel Office Companion	_____	x $21.95 =	$_____

Shipping: Please add $4.50/first book, $1.35/book thereafter; $8.25/book "two-day air," $2.25/book thereafter. For Canada, add $6.50/book.   = $_____

Send C.O.D. (add $4.50 to shipping charges)   = $_____

North Carolina residents add 6% sales tax   = $_____

                                                            Total = $_____

Name _____

Company _____

Address (No PO Box) _____

City_____ State_____ Zip_____

Daytime Telephone _____

___ Payment enclosed ___VISA ___MC Acc't # _____

Expiration Date_____ Interbank # _____

Signature _____

Please mail or fax to: **Ventana Press, PO Box 2468, Chapel Hill, NC 27515**
☎ **919/942-0220, FAX: 919/942-1140**
CAN'T WAIT? CALL TOLL-FREE ☎ 800/743-5369!